Child V

CWLA Standards of Excellence for Child Care, Development, and Education Services

REVISED EDITION

Child Welfare League of America
Washington, DC

The Child Welfare League of America is the nation's oldest and largest membership-based child welfare organization. We are committed to engaging people everywhere in promoting the well-being of children, youth, and their families, and protecting every child from harm.

CHILD WELFARE LEAGUE OF AMERICA, INC.

HEADQUARTERS

440 First Street, NW, Third Floor, Washington, DC 20001-2085

E-mail: books@cwla.org

CURRENT PRINTING (last digit)

10 9 8 7 6 5 4 3 2 1

Cover and text design by Jennifer R. Geanakos

Edited by Eve Malakoff-Klein and Julie Gwin

Printed in the United States of America

ISBN-13: 978-1-58760-075-3

ISBN-10: 1-58760-075-7

Contents

foreword

Setting standards and improving practice in all child welfare services have been major goals of the Child Welfare League of America (CWLA) since its formation in 1920. With the issuance of this revision, CWLA reaffirms its commitment to establishing standards of excellence that can be used as goals to advance and guide contemporary practice. As we continue to learn more about the essentials for the healthy growth of children, families, and communities, CWLA can help to redefine the responsibility of society to provide for children the conditions and opportunities that support their development.

Since the inception of its program of standards development, CWLA has formulated a series of standards based on current knowledge, children's developmental needs, and tested ways of meeting these needs most effectively. The preparation of standards involves an examination of current practices and the assumptions on which they are based, a survey of the professional literature and standards developed by others, and a study of the most recent experiences of social work and related fields— child development, child care, education, mental health, psychology, medicine, psychiatry, and sociology—as well as other appropriate and pertinent fields such as management, business, technology, communication, and marketing, as they bear on child welfare practice and management.

The final formulation of standards follows an extended discussion of principles and issues by experts in each service area, the drafting of a preliminary statement, and a critical review by CWLA member agencies, representatives of related professions, and other national organizations.

CWLA's preparation of standards involves the wide participation of local, state, and national agency representatives. Many CWLA member agencies, including state human service departments as well as private agencies, have contributed the professional time and travel costs of their staff members who developed these standards, reviewed draft statements, and made suggestions for revision. Representatives of national organizations, governmental agencies, sectarian agencies, universities, and professional associations in related fields have taken part in the various committees.

Purpose of CWLA Standards

CWLA standards are intended to be standards of excellence—goals for the continuing improvement of services for children and their families. They are not the criteria for CWLA membership, although they do represent those practices considered to be most desirable in providing services to children and their families. As goal standards, they reflect what we as a field collectively recognize as the best ways to work with children and their families. They provide us with a vision to which we can aspire. They also are used in the development of the standards of accrediting organizations.

CWLA standards are directed to all who are concerned with the enhancement of services to children and their families, including parents; public and private child welfare agency governing board members; direct service, supervisory, and administrative staff members; child health care providers, the general public; citizen groups; public officials; courts and judges; legislators; professional groups; organizations serving children and their families; organizations whose functions include the planning and financing of community services; state or local agencies entrusted by law with functions relating to the licensing or supervision of organizations serving children and their families; tribal organizations; advocacy groups; and federations whose membership requirements involve judgments on the nature of services rendered by their member agencies.

Standards of excellence can stimulate the improvement of services only as they question the value of present practices, convey a conviction that change is desirable, offer a philosophic base from which to examine current practice, and provide a vision toward which we can aim. They provide the means to test the premises from which practice develops and allow the measurement of current services and performance against what is known to be the best possible practice.

Standards are of use in planning, organizing, and administering services; in establishing state and local licensing requirements; and in determining requirements for accreditation. They offer content for teaching and training in child welfare and other related fields, in professional schools, in inservice training and staff development programs, and in the orientation of the organization's governing body members, staff members, and volunteers. They can help to explain and justify expenditures and budget requests to fundraising bodies and appropriation committees of legislatures.

Finally, national standards can promote greater uniformity and consistency across states and local jurisdictions by creating a collective understanding of how a service may more effectively meet the needs of children and their families, what it should be expected to do, and how it can be used. In that way, standards promote increased public interest, understanding, and support for pertinent legislation, improved financing, and the provision of quality services to children and their families.

Development of CWLA Standards

To maintain their visionary quality, CWLA standards are subject to continual review and revision, because knowledge about children, families, communities, human behavior, and the treatment of human needs continues to grow. Developments in management and the social sciences; the continuing evaluation of the effectiveness of current social service practices, policies, and programs; and shifting patterns of social values and social organizations lead to the continued modification of the vision for quality in child welfare practice and management.

The Committee on CWLA *Standards of Excellence for Child Care, Development, and Education Services* met for the first time in July 2002 to begin the process of reviewing CWLA's current standards and to suggest additions or revisions. The committee was composed of individuals representing CWLA public and private member agencies from various geographic regions of the country, researchers, and representatives of national organizations concerned with continually improving the quality of child care services.

The committee began with the framework established in the 1992 volume and crafted standards that built on the philosophy, values, and practice recommendations of the earlier work. The committee held two additional meetings, circulated and reviewed drafts of chapters, and received a draft of the revised volume in March 2004 for review and comment. CWLA's board of directors approved the content of the final draft on May 23, 2004. It henceforth stands as CWLA's policy for the provision of child care, development, and education services.

Standards from an International Perspective

CWLA standards are frequently requested by international officials and child welfare professionals and advocates from other countries who are interested in learning what is considered best practice in North America in a range of practice areas. CWLA standards have been used in developing and improving services in a number of countries, and CWLA's *Standards of Excellence for Adoption Services* (2000) were used as a reference for the development of the Hague Convention Regulations on Intercountry Adoption. CWLA promotes best child welfare practices and supports the enhancement of children's rights throughout the world. Consistent with this effort, we find these standards to be compatible with and supportive of the UN Convention on the Rights of the Child, a blueprint for ensuring children's well-being and protections as a matter of right everywhere.

Bringing CWLA Standards to the Field

These revised standards represent a large step forward in our thinking and practice with regard to child care, development, and education services. They emphasize the importance of providing a range of supports and services for children and their families within a community context. Building upon the previous standards, they describe the unique features of the various types of child care services and settings as well as describing the support services needed to meet the needs of children and their families. The standards also suggest that providers of child care, development, and education services have a critical role to play in ensuring a continuum of services that meets the multiple needs of vulnerable children and families. The standards are consistent with the CWLA National Framework, which envisions a world in which the universal needs of children are met through caring families, communities, and systems.

The revised standards call on professionals and citizens alike to work together to provide the highest quality services, so that every child, young person, and family is strengthened by the service experience and helped to move forward with their lives. We encourage agencies, practitioners, advocates, and concerned citizens to use the standards as a vehicle for pursuing these important goals.

GEORGE W. SWAN, III
Board Chair
Child Welfare League of America, Inc.

SHAY BILCHIK
President/CEO
Child Welfare League of America, Inc.

Acknowledgments

To all those organizations that contributed their time and resources to enable their representatives to participate in this revision process, the Child Welfare League of America (CWLA) expresses its most sincere appreciation. Special appreciation is due to committee chair Rosa Underwood, for her excellent leadership, good humor, and guidance throughout the process, and to all members of the committee for their patience, perseverance, and willingness to go the extra mile to achieve this consensus document. CWLA would also like to acknowledge and thank CWLA intern Katie Durbin, an early childhood education major at the University of Virginia, for her incredible work, which helped the revision process immensely.

We applaud the members of the advisory committee for their vision and assistance to CWLA in assuring the highest quality standards of child welfare practice.

Committee on CWLA Standards of Excellence for Child Care, Development, and Education Services*

Chair: Rosa Underwood, Thompson Children's Home, Charlotte, NC

Phillip Acord, Children's Home Southern Early Childhood Association, Chattanooga, TN

George Askew, American Academy of Pediatrics, Takoma Park, MD

* Agency affiliation at the time the standards were written.

Patricia Beresford, Inwood House, New York, NY

Juanita Cammon, Family and Child Services of Washington, DC, Washington, DC

Michael Cheek, Division of Child Care, Frankfort, KY

Judy Collins, NCCIC State Technical Assistance, Norman, OK.

Teresa DeBoise, Children's Friend and Service, Central Falls, RI

Jack Downey, The Children's Shelter, San Antonio, TX

Deborah Eaton, National Association for Family Child Care, Spring Valley, CA

Gwen Forte, The Children's Home Society of New Jersey, Lakewood, NJ

Colleen Gallagher, Community Coordinated Care for Children, Inc., Orlando, FL

Gloria Gray, Children and Families of Iowa, Des Moines, IA

Jeanetta Green, Alabama Department of Human Resources, Child Day Care Partnership, Montgomery, AL

Andrea Lynn Grimaldi, Zero To Three, Washington, DC

Thomas Gullotta, Child and Family Agency of Southeastern Connecticut, New London, CT

Giuliana M. Halasz, Professional Association for Childhood Education, San Francisco, CA

Terrie Hare, Child Care & Development Office of Child and Family Services, Columbus, OH

Mary Louise Hemmeter, University of Illinois, Champaign, IL

Sharon Huang, I Am Your Child Foundation, New York, NY

Beverly Jones, Fulton County Department of Family and Children Services, Atlanta, GA

Linnea Klee, Children's Council of San Francisco, San Francisco, CA

Rebecca Koffler, Day Care Program, Jewish Child Care Association, Rego Park, New York

Linda Likins, Early Childhood Initiative, Devereux Foundation, Villanova, PA

Peter Michael Miller, America Academy of Pediatrics, San Anselmo, CA

Jayne Pietrass, Council on Accreditation, New York, NY

Michael Pome, Milwaukee County Department of Human
Services, Milwaukee, WI

Hector Luis Ramirez, Para Los Ninos, Los Angeles, CA

Jakob T. Raskob, Child and Family Resources, Inc., Tucson, AZ

Brenda Coakley Rouse, U.S. Department of Health and
Human Services/Child Care Bureau. Washington, DC

Deborah Russo, Department of Children and Families,
Tallahassee, FL

Nancy Schwachter, Caliber Associates, Fairfax, VA

Joyce Shortt, National Institute on Out of School Time,
Wellesley College, Wellesley, MA

Deborah Smolover, I Am Your Child Foundation,
Washington, DC

Kathy Stegall, DHS/Division of Child Care and Early
Childhood Education, Little Rock, AR

Juan Taveras, The Committee for Hispanic Children
and Families, New York, NY

Debbie C. Thomas, Alabama Department of Human Resources,
Montgomery, AL

Aida Veras, Ibero-American Action League, Inc.,
Rochester, NY

Ilene Wilkins, UCP of Central Florida, Orlando, FL

Kristina Young, NSACA, Dorchester, MA

CWLA Staff

Bruce Hershfield, Director, Child Care and Development Services

Pamela Day, Director, Child Welfare Standards

Eve Malakoff-Klein, Director, Publications

Kate Durbin, CWLA Intern

Carrie Martin, Program Manager, Child Welfare Standards

Margie Fowler, Program Assistant, Child Care and Development
Services

Carrie McVicker Seth, Research Analyst

John Sciamanna, Senior Government Affairs Associate

Julie Gwin, Editor

How to Use
CWLA Standards

CWLA standards employ a two-part format designed for quick and easy access to pertinent information. One volume, CWLA *Standards of Excellence for the Management and Governance of Child Welfare Organizations* (1996), presents the generic components of child welfare practice that apply across the field. The components of each specific service are presented in separate volumes and encompass only those service elements applicable to a particular arena of child welfare practice. Each is updated on a regular basis.

The contents page of each standard affords a rapid overview of the general and specific subjects covered. For information on a particular practice, the index lists in alphabetical order each subject of interest and its related categories in the text. Each standard is designated by a number. The digit before the decimal point indicates the chapter in which the standard can be found; the digits after the decimal point designate its numerical order within the chapter. The first (nonindented) paragraph of each numbered section represents the standard. The rest of each section may be considered as elaboration, explanation, or illustration. The introductory chapter affords an historical background and philosophical overview, and provides perspective for the remainder of the volume.

Various aspects of an issue may be discussed in more than one volume of CWLA's standards, and the reader is urged to consult those volumes as appropriate. In addition to this volume on child care, development, self-sufficiency, and education services, CWLA's standards series includes volumes addressing services for:

- adoption,
- child protection,
- family foster care,
- family support and preservation,
- health care for children in out-of-home care,
- in-home aides,
- independent living,
- kinship care,
- pregnant and parenting adolescents, and
- residential care.

Information on these volumes is available from CWLA at the address listed on the copyright page of this volume or online at www.cwla.org.

Differentiation of CWLA Standards of Excellence, Accreditation Standards, and State Licensing

CWLA Standards of Excellence

The Child Welfare League of America standards of excellence are intended to be used as goals for practice in the field of child welfare services. They are intended to provide a vision of what is best for children and their families and, as such, encourage the continual strengthening of services. CWLA standards carry no implication of control or regulation. Rather, by bringing together the collective experience of the field to bear upon the work of each organization, they provide a valuable tool for both public and private agencies.

The standards present practices considered to be most desirable in providing services, regardless of an organization's auspices or setting. CWLA's standards are widely used to influence practice throughout North America and internationally.

CWLA standards of excellence make it possible to compare what exists with what is considered most desirable for children and

their families, and to judge the extent to which current performance approximates or deviates from the most desirable practice. The standards have an educational purpose as well, disseminating what is accepted to be the best current thinking and
practice in each child welfare service area.

Since CWLA initiated its standards-setting function, it has continued to revise established standards and to develop new ones
as new services emerge. Setting standards involves consultation with national experts and direct service practitioners, a
comprehensive review of the literature, and the achievement
of professional consensus based on knowledge, experience, and
research.

Accreditation Standards

Published by accrediting organizations, accreditation standards
constitute a set of requirements for current agency administration, management, and service delivery. They are rigorous but
realistic descriptions of practice standards that a competent
provider organization should be able to meet. They establish a
system based on measurable criteria.

State Licensing

Through the licensing of child-placement agencies, residential
group care facilities, family foster homes, and child day care
facilities, states exercise their police power to protect children
from risks against which they would have little or no capacity
for self-care and protection. Police power, as defined by Black's
Law Dictionary (§1401), is "the exercise of the sovereign right
of the government to promote order, safety, health, morals, and
the general welfare within constitutional limits and is an at-
tribute of government using the power of the state to enforce
laws for the well-being of its citizens." It is the basis of licensing laws. Licensing requirements establish the expectation to
provide basic protections by the state for the well-being of children and their families.

Introduction

The face of families and the organizations that serve them has changed over the past 50 years, adjusting to changes in social and economic forces. Today, a majority of families with children rely on child care services to care for their children during some part of the 24-hour day, whether in full-day child care centers for infants and preschoolers, programs for school-aged children, or family child care homes. All children and families, especially those at risk because of poverty, challenges in family life, or similar difficulties, benefit from high quality child care services.

CWLA's *Standards of Excellence for Child Care, Development, and Education Services* emphasize the importance of making quality, developmentally appropriate child care services available to all families that can benefit from them. These standards recognize that all children have the same basic developmental needs and should have equal opportunities to benefit from advancements in the fields of child development, early childhood education, health care, nutrition, and family support. All children should have developmentally and culturally appropriate experiences while in care, regardless of the emphasis of the child care program, the reason parents use it, or the number of hours children participate in it.

Assumptions and Values

The following assumptions and values form the foundation for effective child care, development, and education services.

- It is the responsibility of every nation to provide access to affordable, quality child care for each child within its states, provinces, and territories. The progress of a nation depends on the ability of adults to raise their children to manage their own lives, to make reasonable and responsible decisions, to be productive, and to reach their full potential. The child care service is an essential support for families in carrying out these tasks.

- The key to the survival of any civilization is how it cares for its young. The need for child care evolved, in part, out of the demands of a service industry economy. Although parents are the primary caregivers, in a postindustrial, service-oriented society, they can benefit from support services that better enable them to fulfill their parenting role. Child care is one such core support service for parents and for family caregivers.

- Child care has become a major North American "industry" and a recognized social institution. To ensure the quality of these important services, policymakers, administrators, and providers must be guided by standards of excellence.

- Adherence to quality standards is essential for organizations that support parents in the preparation of their children for adulthood. Quality child care strengthens school readiness by supporting a child's cognitive, social, emotional, and physical development. Quality child care promotes self-esteem and confidence and has a positive impact on children as they grow into adulthood. These factors help prevent or reduce the incidence of school failure, school dropouts, youth and adult crime, alcohol and substance abuse, crime, family disintegration, teen births, and child abuse and neglect. The quality child care setting also offers unique opportunities for children to learn tolerance of others and to become comfortable with cultural and ethnic diversity.

Historical Highlights and the Role of the Federal Government

Cahan's historical review of early childhood care and education in the United States describes how two tiers of early childhood programs evolved during the 19th and 20th centuries:

> One tier, rooted in the social welfare system, was driven by
> a desire to reduce welfare payments—with scant attention
> to the needs of the child. This system of custodial "group
> child care" for low-income families was in sharp contrast
> to the second tier—child care rooted in the education sys-
> tem that provided "preschool education" mainly for chil-
> dren of the middle and upper-middle classes.
>
> After World War II, a steady expansion of public kindergar-
> ten programs began to challenge this two-tiered system.
> Head Start arrived in the 1960s (as described below), fol-
> lowed in the 1970s by proposals for federal child care stan-
> dards and expanded child care subsidies for low-income
> families. These decades promised progress toward high
> quality care and education for young children of all ages
> and backgrounds. But public policy reversed this trend in
> the 1980s. Federal child care standards were not imple-
> mented, and funding for subsidized child care diminished.
>
> In the final decade of the 20th century, unprecedented at-
> tention was paid to the needs of low-income children and
> families for more and better early care and education. Sev-
> eral forces encouraged this attentiveness. First, the rapid
> influx of married middle-class women into the labor force
> created a new and powerful constituency that favored gov-
> ernmental initiatives to increase the affordability, availabil-
> ity, and quality of child care services. Second, high-quality
> early childhood programs for poor and minority children
> were widely perceived as a way to break the cycle of pov-
> erty and build the human capital we need to maintain this
> nation's economic leadership into the next century. Third,
> disillusionment with the welfare system—and the sentiment
> that welfare mothers must work if their middle-class coun-
> terparts have to—prompted a new social policy requiring
> many on welfare to work. (Cahan, 1989, pp. v–vi)

Head Start

The Head Start program, which began in 1965 as part of the "War on Poverty," brought a strong focus to meeting the care, development, and educational needs of children in low-income families. Conceived as a comprehensive service model for low-income preschool-age children and their families, the Head Start program has become popular with the American public and consistently receives bipartisan support in Congress. Since its inception, the program has expanded dramatically not only in the number of programs, but also in the scope of services and the target population.

Head Start is administered by the Head Start Bureau within the Administration for Children and Families, U.S. Department of Health and human Services. Nearly one million children were enrolled in the program during FY 2002 (Head Start Bureau, 2003). These children and families received services from 1,570 grantees, in 18,865 Head Start centers and home-based programs around the country, with 47,000 receiving services through the Head Start home-based programs (Head Start Bureau, 2003). Head Start grantees and programs reflect the diversity of the families and communities in which they are located. African American, Hispanic, and Caucasian families constitute the majority of Head Start participants (32.6%, 29.8%, and 28.4%, respectively). American Indians (2.9%), Asians (2%), and Hawaiian/Pacific Islanders (1%), while comprising less than 6% of total Head Start participants, are frequently enrolled in centers and home-based programs located in geographic areas where they are the dominant racial population. In addition, Head Start programs have been specifically developed for American Indians and migrant farm workers.

Although the core Head Start program is designed to serve the needs of low-income families with children aged four and five, the 1994 reauthorization of the Act (P.L. 103-252) created the Early Head Start program to meet the needs of families with children age 3 and younger. Begun as a demonstration project, the Early Head Start program served more than 62,000 children in 650 programs during 2002 (Head Start Bureau, 2003). Operating in 50 states and the District of Columbia, Early Head Start provides programs and family support services designed to address the early childhood development needs in the critical years from birth through age 3.

An enduring strength of Head Start is that the programs are as diverse as their participants and the communities they serve. To ensure both the quality of programs and consistency within the Head Start Program nationally, the U.S. Department of Health and Human Services is required to develop and implement program standards and results-based performance measures to ensure the quality of Head Start. Comprehensive Head Start Program Performance Standards have been implemented in the areas of program services (social, physical, emotional, and educational development; health, nutrition, and family involvement/support services), program governance (parental involvement, local boards of directors, grantee qualifications), and program management (administrative and fiscal management, physical facilities). Revised in 1996, these program performance measures serve not only as the mechanism used to identify how specific programs are performing, but also provide excellent guidance regarding the training and technical assistance needs of Head Start grantees and programs. Within the parameters of the Program Performance Standards, each Head Start grantee and program must tailor its services and activities to not only meet the needs of the local community, but to effectively engage children and parents in the acquisition of the skills essential to healthy childhood development and school readiness.

Role of the Federal Government

Aside from the government's role in Head Start, for years the sole source of federal involvement or funding for child care services and subsidies existed only through Social Services funding that was part of the Social Security Act. That funding, which became a block grant in 1981 and was renamed the Social Services Block Grant (SSBG; P.L. 97-35), continued in its role of being the prime federal source of support late into the 1980s. SSBG, however, also funded a range of other human services, including services to the aging, to individuals with disabilities, and to a great number of child welfare services. At times SSBG would be the focal point of national legislative debates to incorporate minimum child care standards. These efforts in the 1970s and 1980s proved unsuccessful as states resisted efforts to have federal mandates in support of child care health, safety and training standards.

In 1988, with the enactment of the Family Support Act P.L. 100-485), specific funding streams were established to provide child care subsidies and services. That act, which incorporated a number of changes to the cash assistance entitlement Aid to Families with Dependent Children (AFDC), created two funding streams for child care, one for families in training and education and a second source of child care entitlement funding for families that left AFDC for work.

In 1990, in a historic move forward for child care, Congress enacted the Child Care and Development Block Grant (CCDBG). Funded at $750 million in its first year, CCDBG specifically targeted child care to low- and middle-income families. Congress also added a limited third funding stream to the AFDC program when it created a capped entitlement for families that were defined as being "at-risk" of going on AFDC. The CCDBG allowed states great flexibility in designing their child care programs. States could use federal funds to provide services to families earning up to 75% of a state's median income level. Families were assured choice in the selection of their providers and both vouchers and contracts could be used to provide services. In addition, CCDBG required states to have in place minimum health and safety standards, although the extent of those regulations were up to each state. CCDBG also created a set-aside of funds that were to be directed toward quality improvement activities and resource and referral.

Child care was a critical element of the debates from 1994 through 1996 when Congress revisited the topic of changes and reforms to the AFDC entitlement and a final welfare bill (P.L. 104-193) was adopted.* When Congress and the President agreed to block grant the cash assistance AFDC program, they also created minimum work requirements for adults receiving benefits, resulting in increased working hours for parents. As a result,

---

* The Personal Responsibility and Work Opportunity Reconciliation Act (PRWORA) of 1996 replaced the Aid to Families with Dependent Children Program with the Temporary Assistance for Needy Families (TANF) program.

more child care funding became a necessary component to any final agreement.

The Temporary Assistance for Needy Families (TANF) block grant also included a major reconfiguration of the nation's child care funding and as a result, a reconfiguration and expansion of state systems. All three AFDC-related child care funds were combined along with the CCDBG funds into one block grant. The new Child Care and Development Fund (CCDF) provided states with regular funding that is distributed through a complex formula that allows states to draw most of their funds by maintaining a minimum state spending level (referred to as the child care Maintenance of Effort or MOE). In addition, each state is eligible to draw down more federal child care funding if it is willing to match a portion of the federal dollars with state dollars. CCDF still required states to have in place minimum health and safety standards. Despite the close tie to the changes in the national welfare system, Congress still maintained the program's mission of providing child care for lower and middle income families by raising the maximum income level of the families state could serve. Congress raised the maximum income eligibility from 75% to 85% of a state's median income level (Child Care Development fund, 45 CFR Parts 98 and 99).

From 1997 through 2002, federal funding for CCDF rose from $3 billion to $4.8 billion. In addition, the new flexibility created in the TANF block grant caused states to place as much as $4 billion in TANF funds into child care so that by 2002, $8.5 billion in federal funds was being spent on child care.

The Impact of Changing Social and Economic Conditions on Families and Children

Changing social and economic conditions have had a profound impact on children and families and on the delivery of child care services.

Changing Family Structure

One of the most profound changes in American society over the last three decades has been the change in family structure.

The proportion of single-parent families, blended families, and families in which both parents work outside the home has dramatically increased.

In 1980, about 21% of children in the United States lived in a single parent family. By 2000, 31% of all children were living in a single parent family (U.S. Bureau of the Census, 2003a). Moreover, family structures are sharply divided along ethnic lines. In 2000, 26% of White children, 34% of Hispanic children and 61% of Black children lived with a single parent (U.S. Bureau of the Census, 2003a).

Single parenthood increased significantly during the latter part of the century as a result of an increase in divorce, separation, and births outside of marriage. The number of divorced persons doubled, from 9.9 million in 1980 to 19.8 million in 2000 (U.S. Bureau of the Census, 2003a). Other factors also have affected family formation. Substance abuse and incarceration of parents, among other causes, have led to an increasing number of grandparents and other kin who are providing temporary or long-term care for their relative children. According to the 1997 National Survey of America's Families, 1.8 million children were living with relatives, with neither of the parents present in the home (Ehrle, Geen, & Clark, 2001). Although not unique to single parent and kinship families, such factors as inadequate financial support, lack of access to affordable health care and child care, and stressful relationships with noncustodial parents may place a greater burden on these families in their efforts to care for their children.

Changing Roles and Responsibilities

The number of married couples with children in which both the husband and wife are in the labor force continued to exhibit an upward trend. Over the past 15 years, the number of such families increased from 14.6 million to 17.1 million (U.S. Bureau of the Census, 2001). To accommodate the increasing number of families where both parents work, the roles and responsibilities of family members have changed. Research suggests that mothers, when present in households, still tend to fulfill the primary caregiving role but that the overall time mothers and fathers spend with children and their roles during such time are changing (Bond, Galinsky, & Swanberg, 1998).

In addition, both fathers and mothers work longer hours per week than 20 years ago (three and five hours longer, respectively; Bond et al., 1998). With parents working longer hours, child care arrangements are often strained. A 1997 survey reported an estimated 38% of children had more than one regular child care arrangement each week (Capizzano & Adams, 2000). A 1999 survey found that 10% of 6- to 12-year-olds regularly spent time alone or with siblings younger than 13, while their parents were employed (Sonenstein, Gates, Schmidt, & Bolshun, 2002). When parents are unable to arrange for quality, reliable care and supervision, children and youth are at increased risk.

Changing Demographics

The demographics of families in America are changing due to the mobility of families, immigration, and differential birth rates. Between 2000 and 2001, almost 40 million Americans moved (U.S. Bureau of the Census, 2003b). Not only was there movement within the country, but there was also movement of people from abroad. In 2002, the foreign-born population numbered 32.5 million, representing 11.5% of the U.S. population (Schmidley, 2003). In addition, an estimated 7 million unauthorized immigrants were residing in the United States as of January 2000 (Immigration and Naturalization Service, 2003).

Birth rates in the country have increased slightly after several years of steady decline. The number of births increased almost 4% between 1997 and 2001 (Martin et al., 2002). Over the past several years, the trend in number of births by race and ethnicity has varied. From 1991 to 2001, the number of births to non-Hispanic Whites and to non-Hispanic Blacks declined by 10% and 11%, respectively. During the same period, the number of births for Native Americans, Asians, and Hispanics increased by 8%, 38%, and 37%, respectively (Martin et al., 2002).

With the differing growth of families across race and ethnicity, American families are becoming increasingly diverse. These changes in the race, culture, and ethnicity of families, along with changes in family structure, challenge child care programs to redesign service delivery approaches to better address the needs of diverse families and communities.

Poverty

The economic condition of families today is unstable and it is the young who bear the heaviest burden. In 2001, 16.3% of the children in the United States lived in poverty. Children comprise 25.6% of the total population but represent 35.7% of the poor (Proctor & Dalaker, 2002). The stress created by living in poverty may play an important role in child safety and well-being (Gil, 1970). Parents who experience prolonged frustration in trying to meet their family's basic needs may be less able to cope with even normal childhood behavior problems. Those parents who lack social support in times of financial hardship may be particularly vulnerable (Thompson, 1995).

During times of economic weakness, poor families are hit the hardest. A 25-city survey conducted by the U.S. Conference of Mayors reported that requests for emergency food assistance increased by an average of 19% in 2002. Of the people requesting food assistance, 48% were members of families (children and their parents). During 2002, requests for shelter by homeless families increased by 20%, with 38% of these requests going unmet. In addition, requests for assisted housing by low-income families and persons increased in 88% of the cities surveyed. All of the city officials believed the nation's weak economy would have a negative impact on hunger and homelessness in the future (U.S. Conference of Mayors, 2002).

In addition, changes in federal and state policies have placed new pressures and demands on poor families with children. The Personal Responsibility and Work Opportunity Reconciliation Act (PRWORA) of 1996 (P.L. 104-93), which replaced the Aid to Families with Dependent Children (AFDC) program with the Temporary Assistance for Needy Families (TANF) program, emphasizes personal responsibility and limits government's role in supporting needy families. There is evidence that some families benefited from TANF participation in the early years of implementation, during good economic times.* Other data sug-

---

*   Employment among welfare recipients increased 80% from 1992 (prior to the Act) to 1999. The employment rate of single mothers under the 200% poverty level rose from 44% in 1992 to 59% in 1999 (U.S. DHHS, 2000). The average monthly earnings of employed welfare recipients increased 49% from 1996 to 2001 (U.S. DHHS, 2003b).

gest that many newly employed families are not better off than before.*

Many working families also struggle to make ends meet. According to one survey, one in six nonelderly Americans lived in working poor families in 1996. The primary earners in working poor families held jobs that offered less pay, less stability, and fewer benefits than earners in nonpoor families. More nonpoor families (88.6%) than working poor families (54.3%) received health insurance through an employer. Compared to the nonworking poor, the working poor were less likely to receive Medicaid and food stamps (Acs, Phillips, & McKenzie, 2000). Without outside funding help, low-income families will sometimes spend 20% or more of their incomes on child care alone. The cost of child care often forces low-income families to choose low-quality care or informal care (Schulman, 2000).

Race and Ethnicity

Families of color face added challenges as a result of racial and ethnic discrimination and poverty. Families of color experience racism and are more likely to be poor (Hill, 1999; McAdoo, 1998; Padilla, 1997; Scannapieco & Jackson, 1996; Vega, 1995). The child poverty rate is highest for children of color. In 2001, 30% of Black children and 28% of Hispanic children lived below the poverty level compared with 9% of non-Hispanic White children (Proctor & Dalaker, 2002).

Children of color often attend public schools that are less academically challenging and may live in communities that have increased rates of crime and violence due to poverty, unemployment, and lack of opportunity (Hill, 1999; McAdoo, 1998; Vega, 1995). Families of color face obstacles when seeking sup-

---

*   A survey conducted by the Children's Defense Fund found that 58% of working families were still not earning above poverty wages. Of the families that were no longer receiving TANF, many were not receiving such important noncash supports as food stamps (50%) and child care benefits (less than one-third), and nearly a third reported at least one family member without health insurance (Children's Defense Fund, 2000). The Fifth Annual Report to Congress on the TANF program reported that the employment rate of current and former welfare recipients increased since TANF was enacted but then leveled off and even declined between 2000 and 2001 (U.S. DHHS, 2003b).

port to help them cope with these challenges. In more recent years, they have endured reductions in services, lack of health insurance, inadequate health care, and lengthy waits at publicly funded clinics (McAdoo, 1998; Padilla, 1997; San Miguel, Morrison, & Weissglass, 1998; Scannapieco & Jackson, 1996).

Specific groups face different and individualized challenges. For example, immigrant families must cope with the stresses of acculturation, a lack of English proficiency, issues arising from their immigration status, and generally lower levels of educational and occupational status (Padilla, 1997; Vega, 1995). Yet the experience of each immigrant group and individual within each group will be different.

Because of the diverse needs and experiences of families in the United States, service agencies and providers should take responsibility for knowing and understanding the issues of specific populations and hiring and training staff who can work effectively with them. Agencies must be committed to providing culturally competent services, including services to non-English-speaking families,* and must allocate the resources and organizational supports necessary to ensure that families are served in a culturally competent way.

Substance Abuse

In 2001, an estimated six million children in the United States lived with at least one parent who abused or was dependent on alcohol or other drugs (Office of Applied Studies, 2003). Although substance abuse has been present in families for centuries, the spread of crack cocaine, amphetamines, and other illegal drugs, in combination with the abuse of alcohol, has brought an increasing number of families to the attention of the child welfare system.

---

* Title VI of the Civil Rights Act of 1964 addresses limited English proficiency service provision, including making provisions for communicating with children and families through the medium that is most comfortable for them, ensuring that agency service descriptions are available in the language(s) of populations served, and that workers are trained to be aware of communication styles and patterns that differ by cultural group (Nash & Velazquez, 2003).

Families experiencing substance problems are particularly vulnerable to disruption, including placement of their children in out-of-home care. An estimated 40% to 80% of families in the child welfare system have problems with alcohol and other drugs that are serious enough to affect parenting (Young, Gardner, & Dennis, 1998). Accessible and affordable treatment options are often in short supply, and when available, timeframes for effective treatment may be inconsistent with the permanency needs of children.

Among adults with a mental disorder that impacts their functioning, an estimated 20% were dependent on or abused alcohol or illicit drugs, compared to 6.13% of adults in the general population. As these mental health problems often go untreated, this further complicates the return of children to their families. In addition, children of alcohol and drug-addicted parents are up to four times more likely to develop substance abuse and mental health problems than other children (NACOA, 1998).

Violence

Societal violence has created an additional stressor for children and their families. Children are exposed to violence in their homes, in their communities, and through the media. The impact of exposure to violence depends on various factors such as a child's age, the frequency and type of violence exposure, neighborhood characteristics, community resources, support from caregivers or other adults, previous trauma experience, proximity to the violent event, and familiarity with the victim or perpetrator (Osofsky, 1997).

Bullying also impacts children and youth in a variety of ways. Nearly 30% of all youth ages 11 to 15 have been a victim or perpetrator of bullying. Youth who bully others are more likely to smoke, drink alcohol, and perform poorly in school. Youth who are bullied are often insecure, depressed, and lonely (Nansel et al., 2001).

Although domestic violence has received increased attention in the past 15 years, it remains an issue for families today. In 2001, almost 692,000 incidents of nonfatal violence occurred against a current or former intimate partner. The majority of the victims (85%) were women (Rennison, 2003). Between 1993 and 1998, almost 70% of intimate partner violence against men and against women occurred at or near the victim's home. Children under 12 years old lived in 43% of the households where intimate partner violence occurred (Rennison & Welchans, 2000).

The presence of domestic violence is a significant factor in parental functioning. It also plays a role in child maltreatment and in the emotional well-being of children now and in the future. Parents who are victims of domestic violence need sensitive and skilled support and assistance in addressing domestic violence issues and maintaining their children's safety. Families that have learned patterns of violence will need assistance to learn new patterns of interaction. Families also can benefit from mutual support (including victim support groups and more generic parent and youth support groups); assistance in meeting housing, health, and other basic needs; and opportunities to participate in normalizing experiences, such as recreation, meals, and social time.

Incarcerated Parents

In 1999, approximately 721,500 state and federal prisoners were parents to 1.5 million children under the age of 18. From 1991 to 1999, the number of minor children with a parent in prison rose by 500,000. Prior to their incarceration, 46% of parents were living with their minor children (Mumola, 2000).

Children of incarcerated parents disproportionately live in poverty and their parents' incarceration makes the situation worse (Wright & Seymour, 2000). One-third of mothers (31%) and 4% of fathers in prison had been living alone with their children prior to their arrest (Mumola, 2000).

Mental Health

An estimated 22% to 23% of the U.S. population (about 44 million people), have diagnosable mental disorders in a given year (U.S. DHHS, 1999). Women experience depression about 1.5 to

3 times more frequently than men. Major depression can affect a mothers' ability to respond to her children and is a risk factor for children experiencing developmental difficulties (Lennon, Blome, & English, 2001).

Children who have a parent with mental illness are at significantly greater risk for multiple psychosocial problems. Rates of child psychiatric diagnosis among children of parents with mental illness are 30% to 50% greater than those of the general child population. Children whose parents have a mental illness may show more developmental delays, fewer academic competencies, and difficulty with social relationships (Nicholson, Biebel, Hinden, Henry, & Stier, 2001).

The mental health of children and youth is also a critical issue. In the United States, four million children and youth suffer from a major mental illness that significantly impairs functioning at home, at school, and with peers (U.S. Public Health Service, 2000). Yet, between 75% and 80% of children and youth do not receive the mental health specialty services they need (U.S. DHHS, 1999). Nowhere is this more evident than for the children who have been placed in out-of-home care. Research shows that more than 80% of children in foster care have developmental, emotional or behavioral problems (Kaplan & Sadock, 2000). In addition, youth suicide continues to be the third leading cause of death among youth 15 to 24 in the United States. Among people ages 15 to 19 years, firearm-related suicides accounted for 62% of the increase in the overall rate of suicide from 1980 to 1997 (Centers for Disease Control, 2001).

Rates of adolescent pregnancy and juvenile delinquency have declined in recent years, yet they continue to remain issues for many families today. Overall, the birth rate for teenagers fell 26% from 1991 to 2001. Teenage birth rates continued to decline for non-Hispanic White, non-Hispanic Black, and Hispanic teenagers. Yet, in 2001, there were almost 446,000 births to adolescents ages 15 to 19 years old (Martin et al., 2002). Children of teen mothers are more likely to have lower birth weights, to perform poorly in school, and to be at greater risk of abuse and neglect (Maynard, 1996; George & Lee, 1997; Wolfe & Perozek, 1997).

The Strengths and Resiliency of Families, Children, and Youth

The social and economic conditions described above can compound and intensify other challenges families are experiencing, such as the death or illness of a spouse or other family member, the loss of a job, mental or physical illness, the disability of a parent, the loss of support from relatives or friends, or the unmet developmental needs of a parent. How families fare, and how well they are able to manage and safely care for children, depends on many things, including the availability of family and community supports and the strengths, resources, and resiliency of the family.

Although families face many challenges, they also possess many strengths and resources, including their own cultures. Families possess protective factors, that is, strengths that enable them to successfully adapt to stressful life events or circumstances. Examples of protective factors include the ability to endure hardship, love for children, capacity to nurture, cooperation with agency and other helpers, knowledge of what a parent should do, ability to delay gratification, and the ability to be assertive (Cole, Day, & Steppe, 1994).

In addition, Hodges (1995) presents a list of personal characteristics and skills that serve as protective factors in children and youth. Examples of personal protective factors in children and youth include:

- responding quickly to danger;
- creating and nurturing relationships that will provide support in times of crisis;
- desiring to learn as much as possible about potentially harmful people or situations;
- exhibiting behavior that is more mature than the expected age; and
- possessing a positive, hopeful attitude that protects against negativism and depression.

Resiliency can be defined as the ability to "bounce back from stress and crisis" (National Network for Family Resiliency, 1996). Resilient children and youth, who can overcome risks and adversity, often exhibit the following traits:

- social competence (responsiveness, cultural flexibility, empathy, communication skills, sense of humor);
- problem solving (planning, help-seeking, critical and creative thinking);
- autonomy (sense of identity, self-efficacy, task mastery, self-awareness, distancing from negative messages and conditions); and
- a sense of purpose and belief in a bright future (goal direction, educational aspirations, optimism, faith and spiritual connectedness) (Benard, 1999).

The communities and cultural experiences of families also provide a reservoir of strength and support. Often people do not recognize strengths and attributes of cultures different from their own. For example, families of color and immigrant families draw on relationships with extended family members as a means of social support. Families of color and different cultures also derive strength from their strong religious orientations and their connection to religious institutions and communities (Cross, 1998; Hill, 1999; McAdoo, 1998; San Miguel et al., 1998).

Community Responsibility for Children and Families

Although families have the primary responsibility for protecting and raising children, communities also are central to the health and well-being of children. Communities provide the context for daily life, the cultural lens for translating information and experience, and the network of supports and connections that help children and young people to overcome difficulties and become contributing members of society. Communities can assist families by making supports and services widely available and by making children and families a priority when making planning, funding and policy decisions. Communities can ensure that children are provided the opportunity for safe, healthy exploration and learning to support their ongoing development.

It is in the best interest of communities to protect children and support families. Healthy children and families give back to their communities in both tangible and intangible ways. They contribute to the vitality and longevity of the community itself and enhance the quality of life for those living in the community. The community as a whole must invest in the supports and services required to ensure the well-being of all of its children and their families, including those who could benefit from residential services.

Moving to a Community, Neighborhood-Based Approach to Supporting All Children and Their Families

In the last decade, increasing attention has been given to the context that families find themselves in—their neighborhoods and communities—and how communities can be mobilized to support and strengthen families. This move in the direction of an inclusive, participatory approach to supporting families and protecting children is an affirming one. It recognizes what is already working well in families and communities and is consistent with CWLA's *Framework for Community Action* (Morgan, Kaplan, & Spears, 2003).

CWLA's *Framework for Community Action* is a resource to support agencies and communities in improving child and family well-being. The Framework envisions "an America where every child is healthy and safe and where all children develop to their potential," becoming adults who are "able to make positive contributions to family, community, and the nation." Children and youth have five universal needs that must be met to ensure their survival and to promote their healthy development:

- *Basic needs* such as proper nutrition, economic security, adequate shelter and clothing, a basic education, and prevention and primary health and mental health care.

- *Nurturing relationships* with parents, kin, and other caregivers; caring relationships with community members; and good relationships among children and youth themselves.

- *Opportunities and experiences* that motivate and equip children to succeed; opportunities to develop talents and skills, to contribute to their families and communities, and to make positive connections to their cultures, traditions, and spiritual resources; early assessment and intervention to prevent later, more serious problems.

- **Protection from harm** such as abuse and neglect by their caregivers, as well as witnessing or being victimized by family, school, or community violence; protection from the harms of discrimination, media violence, Internet victimization, environmental toxins, and accidental injury.
- **Easing of the impacts of harm** through ensuring immediate and ongoing safety, supplying immediate and continuing emotional support, assessing the need for and providing medical, mental health, and other needed services, and making amends through restorative justice practices (Morgan et al., 2003).

To meet the universal needs of all children requires people working together in a comprehensive approach, guided by a common set of principles. These core principles should guide agencies' and communities' actions on behalf of children and youth:

- **Supporting families**: By supporting families in nurturing their children, professionals and community members can help to ensure that parents, other relatives and caregivers have the skills and resources to raise healthy and well-adapted children.
- **Promoting prevention**: Programs and practices that nurture and protect children in their earliest development, which prevent abuse and neglect, and that detect and intervene at the earliest possible indication of risk should be available to all families.
- **Advancing social justice**: All children, regardless of gender, ability, economic status, and ethnic, racial, spiritual, and cultural background, have an equal right to have their universal needs met. All community partners can advocate for the ideals and values of social justice both locally and globally.
- **Working collaboratively**: When people come together, collective capacities emerge that individual partners did not possess. Communities can harness this synergy to solve shared problems and work toward the common good.
- **Respecting and valuing diversity**: Diverse cultures, traditions, and perspectives are sources of strength

and creativity that community partners can draw upon to nurture healthy families and children.

- *Building capacity*: By recognizing and nurturing the assets and strengths of children, youth, families, and communities, communities tap into sources of energy and creativity that have the greatest potential for meeting children's needs and encouraging their optimal growth.

- *Nurturing leadership*: Leadership requires dedication, passion, and a willingness to take risks. It comes from those willing and able to inspire and guide others to get things done on behalf of families and children.

- *Utilizing evidence-based strategies*: Applying knowledge of factors and strategies that contribute to or impede healthy human development can help community partners to design and implement policies, practices, and programs that are effective in helping children to thrive.

- *Measuring results*: Using clear outcome measures to guide and evaluate efforts increases the likelihood that the community's work will result in positive results for children, youth, and families (Morgan et al., 2003, pp. 6–7).

The Role of Child Care Services in the Community Approach to Supporting All Children and Their Families

The child care service provider plays a vital role in ensuring that children and families are provided quality services within a community context, including:

- creating an environment that promotes respect for cultural diversity;
- linking and coordinating effectively with other resources to help children and their families access needed services;
- providing a healthy and safe environment for all children;
- building school readiness;

- promoting children's development and supporting families in caring for their children; and
- advocating for the creation of new services and system changes to meet identified unmet needs.

These roles call upon the child care service provider to be active in promoting and advocating for good parenting and supporting families. The community approach requires the child care service provider to be increasingly involved with other community agencies and institutions that support children and their families, and to take a formal role in service delivery systems. It calls upon the agency to establish formal partnerships across the service system and to take part in galvanizing the relevant agencies in the community to work collaboratively toward the common goal of providing a comprehensive system of services to enable all families to care for their children.

Child Care Service Today

Child care is a service for children that is provided in support of their family, is directed to their healthy growth and development, and supplements the care provided within the family.

Purposes of the Child Care Service

The purpose of child care is to supplement the care, attention to the developmental needs, and protection that children receive from their parents. Regardless of the form in which it is delivered, child care should be designed as a developmental service. Developmentally appropriate child care supplies a nurturing environment that cultivates the physical, emotional, intellectual, social, and cultural potential of the child. It also helps all family members pursue their own individual and collective goals.

Child care also serves as a preventive service, including supporting child rearing, helping to manage family stress, preventing illness and injury, promoting health and wellness, and strengthening families and children to avoid family breakdown.

Child care can be designed as a therapeutic service that seeks to heal psychological damage caused by deprivation, discontinuity of care, substance abuse, poverty, homelessness, illiteracy, violence, lawlessness, or tension in the home. Child care can also be used as part of the treatment plan for children with developmental delays, physical disabilities, or emotional disturbances, as well as for medically fragile children and those who have experienced abuse and neglect. Children with such special needs should be served in the least restrictive and/or natural environment as is beneficial, to allow them to receive all appropriate services and to achieve their full potential.

Child Care as a Service for Children and Families

Child care services should be child centered and family focused. Child care programs are designed and staffed to offer group or family care in child care centers, group child care homes, or family child care homes to supplement the childrearing practices and responsibilities of the parents.

Care for children outside the home is provided in many forms and for different purposes. It is used by birth, custodial, foster, or adoptive parents and by guardians for a variety of reasons.

Child care standards help to ensure that those children entrusted to the care of providers receive the supplemental care required for their healthy growth and development.

Goals of the Child Care Service

The goals for every child care service should include:

- meeting the basic needs of children in a safe and nurturing setting that supports healthy growth and development;
- creating a stimulating, developmentally appropriate, early learning environment;
- working together in partnership with and supporting parents in the care of their children;
- serving as an integral part of the community's human service network;
- providing or facilitating access to an array of child and family support services;
- recognizing differences and fostering individualization in all children;

- partnering with health care providers to meet the child's developmental, health, and medical needs;
- establishing a developmentally and culturally appropriate plan for services to each child and periodically evaluating the effectiveness of these services;
- promoting children's self-confidence, curiosity, creativity, and self-discipline;
- providing a supportive environment that encourages children to solve problems, master self-help and learning skills, make decisions, engage in activities, ask questions, explore, and experiment with their environment;
- promoting the self-worth of each child through healthy social and emotional relationships and an awareness of ethnicity and individuation; and
- fostering cooperation and positive social relationships among children and between children and adults.

Components of the Child Care Service

The essential components of a child care service include:

- a definitive, developmentally appropriate program curriculum, including recreational and other age-appropriate programming for school-age children;
- safe and adequate facilities and equipment designed specifically for children;
- a service plan with objectives for each child, developed in conjunction with the family;
- culturally competent staff members trained to help children broaden their awareness, knowledge, language, literacy, and communication skills;
- program diversity to allow for appropriate services for children of different ethnic, economic, social, and cultural backgrounds;
- parent-participation activities, parent education and support services (including program planning assignments and volunteer services), and membership on advisory and policy boards;
- nutritious meals;

- appropriate health policies and practices and activities to develop physical abilities;
- physical activity programs to develop physical abilities and promote gross and fine motor abilities;
- coordination with parents and primary child health care providers to meet the developmental, health, and medical needs of children with special needs;
- social service support provided by the agency or obtained from the community to assist parents and children as needed;
- administrative planning and coordination within the framework, purpose, politics, and goals of the agency board of directors; and
- coordination with other relevant community services.

The Range of Child Care Programs and Settings

A wide range of resources and facilities can be used for the care of children outside the home. Programs will differ according to the needs of the children they serve and the varying responsibilities of providers for the care, protection, development, education, recreation, or treatment of the children.

Today, child care services are provided by nonprofit organizations, social agencies, government agencies, faith-based groups, hospitals, private entrepreneurs, independent family child care providers, employers, labor unions, corporate for-profit chains, schools, and nonsocial welfare government agencies (such as the military; U.S. Congress; federal, state, and local executive departments; and public housing authorities). These agencies provide programs and services whose primary purpose may be child development, education, treatment, or recreation.

Child care can be provided in family child care homes, group child care homes, or child care centers.

- Family child care homes are settings in which an individual adult, sometimes with assistance, provides child care services in her or his private residence for fewer than 24 hours a day, generally for six or fewer children.
- Group child care homes are settings in which two or more adults jointly provide child care services in a

private residence for fewer than 24 hours a day, generally for a group of seven to 12 children.

- Child care centers are settings in which part-day or full-day group programs are provided in nonresidential facilities (e.g., child care center building, social agency, recreational agency, place of worship, school, workplace, public housing, hospital) for seven or more children.

No matter what the setting, basis, or background of the program, it is necessary to ensure that the service given is in the best interests of the individual children, and that the daily experiences they receive are of benefit to them.

Child Care Participation and Facility Data

According to a 1999 survey, nearly 20.5 million children of employed parents are regularly in nonparental care: 8.7 million children four years or younger (about 75%), about 2 million five year olds (about 80%), and 9.8 million school-age children under 13 (50%). In addition, an estimated 10% of children are home alone or with another sibling under 13 while the primary caregiver is at work (Urban Institute, 2002).

According to the Children's Foundation Child Care Licensing Study (2003), 306,802 family child care homes (up from 223,351 in 1990) and 116,409 child care centers (up from 86, 212 in 1991) are licensed in the United States. Because many providers are unlicensed and do not show up in state or local information systems, the number of regulated child care providers is assumed to represent only a small percentage of the total number of such providers.

Trends, Recent Research, and Findings

Research findings in the field of early child development over the past 10 years have implications for the child care service industry. Based on these findings, child care experts are increasingly placing emphasis on the earliest years of life as key to a child's development and reviewing their practices to provide for the optimal development of children in their care.

Early Brain Development and Early Literacy

At birth, an infant's brain contains neurons that exist mostly separately from one another. Connections between these neurons will be made over the first few years of life and experience plays a primary role in determining which neural connections will be formed and subsequently stay strong and which will be eliminated in early childhood (Gable, 2002). These early experiences and connections lay the foundations for emotional health, intelligence, and even moral development (Shonkoff & Phillips, 2000).

Predictable and supportive care is essential to the development of key neuron connections. Care that is withdrawn, unresponsive, angry, or abusive can lead to the development of synapses that lead to similar behavior in the child. Research has shown the benefits in making the most of daily routines and building relationships with young children. Care providers are advised to learn to read children's emotions and respond quickly and appropriately to their needs. In addition, efforts should be made to provide each child with a primary caregiver who does not change. Care providers should also recognize each child's developmental stage and work to enhance development.

Language and literacy development also begin in the first three years of life and are closely linked to the child's early experiences, especially exposure to reading and speaking (Rice, Burkes, & Kaplan-Sanoff, 2001). Literacy for infants, toddlers, and young children does not refer to the ability to read but instead to an overall understanding and mastery of language skills. These skills are best developed through exposing the child to positive interactions with adults and other children involving storytelling activities, music, verbal communication, and literacy materials such as books, markers/crayons, and paper.

School Readiness

School readiness is a child's readiness to enter the mainstream school system and face the challenges posed by it, beginning with kindergarten. Since 1998, educators and government policymakers have focused on increasing the school-preparedness of America's preschoolers. A longitudinal analysis, *The Children of the Cost, Quality, and Outcomes Study Go to School* (Peisner-

Feinberg et al., 1999), showed that students who attended higher quality child care centers were more prepared cognitively (math and language skills) and socially (interactions with peers, problem behaviors) for the transition to school (Peisner-Feinberg et al., 1999). The influence of quality child care on school readiness held true across a wide range of family and economic backgrounds. The strength of the teacher-child relationship influenced social skills, while the quality of the classroom was related to the cognitive skills. Increasingly, child care providers are directing their developmentally appropriate curriculum to enhancing the preparedness of children for school.

Universal Preschool

Related to the issue of school readiness is the idea of universal preschool. This movement to provide publicly funded prekindergarten (pre-K) programs to all four-year-old children has come about in response to the growing volume of research that shows that children who are cognitively and socially prepared for kindergarten generally do better throughout their school career than those unprepared. Many states have already implemented universal preschools, which are currently state-funded and controlled. For example, through its Parental Choice program, Georgia now educates 70% of its 4-year-olds in their universal preschool program funded by lottery sales (Schumacher, Greenberg, & Lombardi, 2001).

Universal preschool remains a controversial issue. Concerns include:

- the funds needed to support universal preschool may divert needed assistance away from low-income families in need of child care for children under age four and for school-aged children;

- how to balance the use of both public and private preschool services including the use of family and group child care homes; and

- whether the universal preschool services will continue to be part-day, part-year programs that leave working families needing to find appropriate child care for the remainder of the day or year.

Also, as more research about the importance of development from zero to three emerges, questions are being raised about the efficacy of funding only programs for four-year-olds as a way to increase school readiness.

Tiered Strategies for Quality (Tiered Licensing/Tiered Reimbursement)

With the increased emphasis on creating quality child care centers and family child care homes, many states have created programs and strategies to increase the number of these high quality settings and increase enrollment of low-income children in such programs. As of November 2002, 34 states, including the District of Columbia, had implemented some kind of tiered strategy for improving child care programs and family child care homes. These strategies rate each center based on its level of quality: those meeting basic licensing requirements receive the lowest rating (e.g., one star) and those meeting nationally recognized accreditation standards and higher state-issued standards receive higher ratings (e.g., three stars). Tied to these scales is usually some form of reimbursement formula that ensures that programs with the highest ratings receive the highest level of reimbursement from the state (National Child Care Information Center, 2002).

Accreditation

Accreditation offers another way to promote higher quality child care programs. The process of accreditation, offered by national and state organizations, involves the evaluation of every aspect of the child care program and clear goal setting for continued quality improvement. Accreditation standards are developed from the most current research and recommendations from the child care, early child development, and child health fields.

Staff (Workforce Recruitment, Retention, and Professional Development)

An effort to increase the training, credentials, and wages of child care providers has emerged in response to research that shows that center quality can be directly linked to the education level of the child care providers as well as the staff-turnover rate.

Quality child care centers develop and use recruitment practices and job descriptions that clearly explain the educational and training requirements and expectations for staff.

Currently only 18 professions report lower average wages than child care providers (Bureau of Labor Statistics; Occupational Employment Statistics), despite the importance of the task they perform. Many child care centers advocate for funding to increase wages and work to set up compensation packages that include benefits (including time release to take classes and health and retirement benefits) and the potential for raises and promotions based on educational attainment and/or length of employment.

Some states have implemented programs that provide funding to help child care providers to increase their knowledge and skills by taking classes and earning various degrees in early childhood development. The programs also may provide qualified substitute care providers for participants while they are attending class, and salary enhancements or bonuses when they return to their child care jobs because of their improved qualifications. T.E.A.C.H (Teach Education and Compensation Helps) Early Childhood® Project, started in North Carolina and now implemented in other states, funds such scholarships and raises to child care providers at state-licensed centers. In addition, other programs, like Child Care WAGE$® Project (also in North Carolina), provide wage supplements to child care providers who meet certain educational and time-commitment requirements and work in centers that meet county or state regulations. Such programs provide the necessary benefits and opportunities for staff and result in improved recruitment and retention of qualified staff.

Technology

The rise of computer technology and the advent of the Internet have affected the child care industry as they have other aspects of contemporary life. Child care providers can now go online to take classes, participate in distance learning programs, and earn degrees or advance their knowledge in early childhood education and development. Computers can be used, as developmentally appropriate, as education tools in the classroom and in the home, supplementing learning with educational games and research tools. Centers and family child care homes can develop websites posting information about services, accreditation, and the like. Parents can access information on local child care services such as Child Care Resource and Referral organizations and selection criteria.

Multiage Groupings

Family child care uses multiage groupings, a concept now being used in limited way in child care centers. Limited research on multiage groupings for preschoolers has shown that it increases academic and social skills in young school-age children, but more research is needed (Kinsey, 2001). The most important consideration in any classroom, no matter its composition, is the developmental needs of the children.

Behavior Management/Challenging Behavior

Child care providers/programs must address an increasing number of challenging behaviors in the children they serve. Prevention and intervention programs initiated in early childhood can produce dramatic improvements in children who have or are at risk of developing challenging behavior (Smith & Fox, 2003). In working with this population, child care service providers should coordinate with other local agencies and primary health care providers to form a cohesive child guidance and behavioral management system that takes into account the needs of the family, the individual, and personnel, and provides all relevant services necessary to help the child. In addition, providers can assist parents through parent training, coaching, and referral. The child care program can serve as a model for parents by providing an environment that prohibits corporal punishment, verbal abuse, and deprivation, and emphasizes consistent daily routines and clear expectations for children to develop the necessary self-management and social skills (Massachusetts Office of Child Care Services Child Guidance, n.d.).

Childhood Obesity

In 2002, one in five children was overweight—a number that has doubled in the past 30 years (Torgan, 2002). This rise has been blamed on the more sedentary lifestyle led by today's children as a result of more time spent inside watching TV or playing computer/video games. Childhood obesity, which is a problem for both children and adolescents, increases the risk of diabetes, adult obesity, hypertension, sleep apnea, joint problems, and social problems. Many child care providers have made a healthy diet, nutrition, and daily physical activity a key part of their programs.

Inclusion

The Individuals with Disabilities Education Act (IDEA) (P.L. 105-12) guarantees an education and any necessary services to children with disabilities to prepare them to achieve their maximum potential, including employment and independent living, when possible. This law, in conjunction with the ADA (Americans with Disabilities Act), has pushed the movement to include children with special needs in mainstream classrooms and family child care and group child care homes, or what are sometimes called *natural environments*. Inclusion has gained increasing support from experts in the field and researchers, who see the improvements that children with special needs can bring to a quality classroom, including an opportunity to teach tolerance and diversity.

These benefits are augmented when children are included at an early age, taking advantage of the amount of development that takes place in the earliest years. When inclusion services are used in child care programs, parents, providers, and outside specialists are involved in creating, providing, and regularly monitoring a comprehensive service for the development of the child. Providers, however, must be adequately prepared to serve children with disabilities and outside resources may be required to properly implement an inclusion approach.

Better Baby Care Campaign

Due to the increase in the number of infants and toddlers in child care and in response to new findings about the importance of the early years of life in development, a coordinated campaign has emerged to improve the quality of care for children ages birth to 3. This campaign seeks to work in conjunction with already existing federal, state, and local organizations to improve policies governing early child care, parental leave, health care, parent education and related policies. Concerned community members are encouraged to advocate in a variety ways for the policy changes needed to improve the quality of care of infants and toddlers (www.betterbabycare.org).

Funding

Although child care is still viewed by some as exclusively a private family responsibility, a movement has been encouraging new initiatives for a much broader range of financial supports for child care resources. Much of the impetus for this movement comes from findings on early brain development and the importance of providing nurturing, stimulating experiences for infants, toddlers, and preschoolers to ensure later school success.

Parents

The majority of the burden of financing child care falls to parents. Many child care programs provide sliding-scale fees tied to parents' income, but the cost of quality child care continues to rise. In 2000, the cost of child care for a four-year-old averaged $4,000 to $6,000 per year and went as high as $10,000. Costs for younger children are even higher. The cost of child care varies by the age of the child, the type of care provided, and the community. Child care is a significant part of a family's budget regardless of the type of care selected or the community in which the family lives. Without outside funding help, low-income families will sometimes spend 20% or more of their incomes on child care alone (Schulman, 2000).

Local, State, and Federal Governments

The U.S. government provides financial support to families for child care from a variety of sources through state and local governments. The Dependent Care Tax Credit is a credit against the federal income tax for up to 35% of qualified, employment-related, dependent care expenses. A number of states also provide additional dependent care tax credits. In 2000, 6.4 million tax payers applied for the federal credit and received $2.8 billion in tax relief, down from $4.2 billion in claims in 1990.

States have been funding child care assistance in recent years using money primarily from three federal grants: the Child Care and Development Block Grant (CCDBG), the Temporary Assistance to Needy Families (TANF), and the Social Services Block Grant (SSBG). The Child Care and Development Fund (CCDF) provides child care subsidies for families earning up to 85% of their state's median income. Federal CCDF funds in 2002 were $4.8 billion. Up to 30% of TANF funds can be transferred to CCDF or spent directly on child care (Internal Revenue Service, 2000). Under federal guidelines, states set guidelines for child care policies and decide which families will be served. They are not required to guarantee child care service to anyone. Funding priorities have shifted with an increased emphasis on assisting families transitioning to work pay for child care. As a result of these shifting priorities, other low-income families have not been included in the assistance packages in some states (GAO-03-588).

In addition to these resources, the government provides funding for the Child and Adult Care Food Program through the U.S. Department of Agriculture. This program provides funding to purchase food and to provide nutritional information to eligible child care programs.

Separate appropriations from the U.S. Department of Health and Human Services fund the Head Start and Early Head Start programs that provide early childhood education services for the most severely disadvantaged children, as described above.

Employers

Most employers do not provide child care or child care subsidies for their employees. Many states have provided tax credits for employers to encourage them to create child care programs and sites. In June 2001, the Economic Growth and Tax Relief Reconciliation Act (EGTRRA) was passed, which gives employers a 25% federal credit for the costs of operating, acquiring, or contracting out to a third party child care provider. These tax credits, however, have done little to increase the number of employer-run or subsidized child care centers (FitzPatrick & Campbell, 2002). It is not clear why employers have not begun to provide child care for employees, but it may be that the state tax credits are too small or employers are not aware of them. (The federal tax credit has yet to be evaluated.)

Charities and Organizations

Local and national charities often provide funding or subsidies for child care for low-income and at-risk families. In addition, they fund research in the field of early childhood development and child care. Child care providers and parents may seek charitable donations from local or national charities, whether faith-based or independent, to augment funding from the government and improve the quality of care available to children.

Building a Community-Based System for Child Care

The Community's Responsibility for Its Children

Communities have a stake in the well-being of their children. The future of any society depends on the healthy physical, mental, and emotional development of its children. Because of the value to children of their families, the community has an obligation to support parents in the performance of their child rearing role and to help strengthen family life.

Functions of a Coordinated System

Effective service delivery systems may take different forms in different communities, but they should work together in each community to establish shared purposes, clear definitions of roles and responsibilities, joint planning for resource development, and organized advocacy efforts.

Shared purposes

To achieve an effective local coordinated child care service system, all relevant sectors (including public and private funding sources, providers, parents, resource and referral agencies, community action agencies,

schools, health care systems, and civic organizations)
should assess the need for child care and agree on common purposes. The explicit identification of these
shared purposes is the first step in planning a comprehensive array of child care services.

Clear definitions of roles and responsibilities

In many communities, several providers may be offering the same type of service while none are providing
other needed services, such as child care for ill children, respite care, or care for children with special
needs. Child care providers should define these gaps
in services to enable local communities to maximize
limited resources. To expand the availability of child
care services, providers should clearly define the programs for which each is responsible. In the public sec-
tor, interagency arrangements should be used to focus
the available services on common goals and should be
linked in an organized fashion if children and their
families are to be served effectively.

Joint planning for resource development

Because service resources are often scarce in relation to need, a coordinated child care service system requires agreement among providers about service priorities.

Advocacy

Advocacy on behalf of family needs should be used to
obtain additional resources, change community attitudes, and modify media messages. The child care service should collaborate actively with other participating agencies in organized advocacy efforts that complement other systemwide activities. These activities
should build a constituency for child care in the community, increase public awareness and involvement,
and attract and secure new funding for child care activities. The staff, parents, and providers from the
child care service should participate in the biennial
state planning process for the development of the state
plan to implement the federal child care and development block grant.

Outreach

Some families have not had experience in using child care, do not know how to obtain and use community resources, including the child care service, or may not believe that anyone is interested in them or able to help them. The child care service should make its services known to parents, relevant groups, and the rest of the community. Services should be made available not only to those who request them and are motivated to use them, but also to those in the community who are recognized by others as needing support but are unable to take the initiative to seek it.

Working with Community Groups

Child care service staff members should become familiar with all relevant community resources that can play an important role in supporting families. The child care service should make its services known to relevant agencies and individuals to whom families may turn for support. The child care service should seek cooperation with the media, leadership of ethnic and cultural minority groups, the resource and referral service, child health care providers, neighborhood centers, businesses, unions, self-help groups, and other relevant public and voluntary organizations.

Unmet Needs

The child care service should inform the community of the need for and the costs of providing adequate child care services. The child care service should recognize any deficiencies in the community's child care services and advocate to fill these unmet needs.

Planning New Child Care Facilities

The child care service should help communities address the need for child care services in planning new housing developments or redevelopment projects, in the construction of new public buildings, in planning residential neighborhoods, and in establishment or modification of zoning laws. Space should be provided for child care facilities, when feasible, in existing or new multipurpose structures, such as public housing projects, settlement houses, neighborhoods service centers, community buildings, child health clinics, schools, and faith based organizations. When funds are available to construct a building for a child care facility, members of the community should be consulted in selecting the site to minimize the risk of investing large sums of money in a property location that may be unsuitable. Zoning laws should stipulate the same zoning regulations for child care centers as they do for schools and places of worship. For zoning purposes, family child care homes and group care homes should be considered the same as any other family home, so that they can available in areas where children live.

Scope of the Standards

CWLA's *Standards of Excellence for Child Care, Development, and Education Services* describe best practices in an array of child care settings and programs. The standards present a range of services that should be available to children and families, to assist them in meeting the job, education, and other demands of daily life and, as needed, in addressing challenges that threaten child and family safety and well being. The array of child care services includes center-based care for infants, toddlers, and preschool-age children, family child care and group family child care homes, afterschool programs, Head Start and Early Head Start programs, and part-day preschool centers.

The child care, development, and education program should include both a high-quality developmental learning program and a health, safety, and nutrition program. Chapter 1 of these standards describes the essential components of a high-quality developmental learning program. Chapter 2 describes the necessary ingredients of a health, safety and nutrition program. Chapter 3 describes the service environment for a range of child care services. Chapter 4 addresses all aspects of staffing the child care service. Chapter 5 describes the administrative aspects of child care services. Chapter 6 addresses child care resource and referral services, family child care networks/systems, and child care subsidy systems. Chapter 7 describes the family support, social service, and the mental health service components of a child care program.

The standards are intended for a broad audience, including public and private child and family service agencies, child development agencies, child welfare administrators, state and local policy makers, courts, health, and mental health professionals, legislators, educators, community members, consumers, family members, and all others concerned with building and maintaining healthy children, families, and communities.

1

The Quality Child Care Program

Goals

I. The child care program provides a developmentally appropriate learning experience for all children in care, regardless of the age of the child and the reasons for the care.

II. The daily developmental learning activities in the child care program are planned in accordance with contemporary principles of child development, child care, education, health care, nutrition, recreation, and family support, and with respect for individual and family needs and cultural diversity.

III. Developmental opportunities, designed to meet the individual needs of children, are provided in all areas of growth, e.g., cognitive (especially language development), social, emotional, physical, and character (moral) development.

IV. Children are provided with opportunities to form relationships with other children and adults, to use a variety of materials and equipment, and to increase their levels of self-confidence and mastery.

V. The child care program meets each child's special needs directly or through referral, consultation, or coordination with other service providers.

The child care, development, and education program, re-gardless of the age group served, should include both a high-quality developmental learning program and a health, safety, and nutrition program (see Chapter 2).

1.1   Developmentally Appropriate Learning Program

The child care service should provide a developmentally ap-propriate learning experience for the child, regardless of the child's age, the program's purpose, the reasons child care is used by the parents, or the setting in which care is provided.

When children are regularly away from their homes, it is essential that they receive the care and supervision they need in an environment conducive to developmental learn-ing and to enrichment of their experience in their homes.

In its broadest sense, learning is a lifelong process that be-gins at birth. Developmental learning occurs during every moment of the day, wherever the child is, and whether or not the stated purpose of a given program includes "educa-tion." Developmentally appropriate learning that includes social, emotional, cognitive, physical, and character devel-opment should permeate the child's care experience.

- For young children, play is an indispensable devel-opmentally appropriate learning experience, and the things with which children play are part of their learn-ing environment. From birth to 5 years of age, chil-dren absorb information and experience through their play. The daily program for children under the age of five should reflect an understanding that developmen-tal learning, education, and play are continuously interrelated.

- For school-age children, recreation and activity op-tions should be essential components of the program. Some children may choose cognitive or academic ac-tivities in their afterschool or vacation period, but others will be happier and will learn and develop more readily by participating in a variety of recre-ational activities.

Research into the development of infants, toddlers, and young children has shown the importance of nurturing environments and developmentally appropriate activities in the formation of the brain's neural connections. These findings show the necessity of positive environments and experiences in providing every child in child care with the potential to learn and grow in every aspect of development (e.g. cognitive, social, etc.). Shonkoff and Phillips (2000) concluded that strong nurturing relationships, early intervention programs, positive environments, well-defined goals, and supportive communities and parents should all be key, basic aspects of the child care developmental learning program. For the child who has been deprived of experiences that stimulate intellectual, social, and emotional development, the child care program has an even greater opportunity to supply the necessary developmental learning and socialization experiences.

The developmental learning program should not focus on any one aspect of the cognitive development of the children in its care. Instead, care providers should realize the value of Gardner's (1983) theory of multiple types of intelligence and emphasize all seven types of intelligence. Gardner's theory states that there is no single "intelligence" and we as a society limit ourselves by trying to define intelligence by tests of math and verbal abilities. The seven types of intelligence include (1) visual/spatial intelligence; (2) musical intelligence; (3) verbal intelligence; (4) logical/mathematical intelligence; (5) interpersonal intelligence; (6) intrapersonal intelligence; and (7) bodily/kinesthetic intelligence.

The developmental program should employ materials and strategies (e.g., musical instruments, group games/activities, etc.) that support the development of all of these types of intelligence.

The child care developmental learning program should also be prepared and able to handle children with a wide range of special needs. Children with special needs should be included within the classroom or family child care home of their normal developing peers whenever possible. The same developmentally appropriate activities and materials should be used with them as are used with their peers. Care providers should be specially trained and prepared to appropriately respond to the developmental challenges that children with special needs face.

Parents should be encouraged to continue this developmental learning at home. Through participation in the child care service, parents can become acquainted, through their child's developmental experiences, with new opportunities for enjoyment and learning.

1.2   Planning Developmentally Appropriate Learning Activities

The daily developmentally appropriate learning activities of the child care program should be planned in accordance with contemporary principles of child development, child care, education, health care, nutrition, recreation, and family support, as they define the child's needs and cultural experiences.

Providers who are qualified by appropriate training and experience and compensated accordingly should carry out these learning activities (see Staffing section).

Developmentally Appropriate Learning Principles and Goals Common to All Child Care Programs

The developmentally appropriate learning goals and the content of the child care program should be based on common principles. Child care programs, however, should differ in certain significant aspects in relation to the developmental level and age of the children served, and the hours of attendance in the program.

1.3   Goals of the Developmentally Appropriate Learning Program

The developmentally appropriate learning goals for each child in a child care program should be realized through opportunities to form relationships with other children and adults, to use various materials and equipment, and to increase levels of self-confidence and mastery.

Children in a child care program should have opportunities to:

- receive emotional support, warmth, and caring from others;
- interact with positive adult role models with whom they can identify;
- work with tools or other objects from the natural environment, sometimes in play, sometimes in purposeful pursuits of the real world;
- learn appropriate health practices and nutrition;
- be exposed to literacy materials (e.g., books, writing instruments, etc.) and oral communication (e.g., talking, reading aloud, storytelling) to promote increased language and literacy skills;
- perform a variety of tasks to achieve competence in some self-help skills;
- experience a balance of free space, free time, and free choice;
- experience a combination of adult-directed and child-directed activities;
- assume individual and group responsibilities;
- interact with other children, form friendships, and participate in group fun and planned activities;
- affirm their own heritage and culture and accept and appreciate those of others;
- work at their own developmental level and pace, yet have appropriate challenges;
- learn how to handle success and failure;
- explore, invent, and pursue individualized ideas and interests;
- be exposed to age-appropriate technology and the skills associated with it;
- learn to be a part of a family;
- become fluent in English while maintaining native language skills, where applicable;
- participate in a multisensory environment;
- develop skills necessary for entering public school (for preschool children);
- participate in activities that promote critical thinking, problem solving, and decisionmaking;

- participate in age-appropriate physical activities;
- have any special needs identified and met;
- be exposed to clear "ready to learn" goals for school-age children that go beyond academic skill development; and
- participate in organized recreational activities and individual and team sports (for school-age children).

1.4   Principles for the Developmentally Appropriate Learning Program

The developmentally appropriate learning program of the child care service should be based on knowledge and understanding of the fundamental needs of children.

The program should allow for individualization according to the child's experiences in the home and community. The needs of a given child should determine what is expected of the child and what activities and relationships with other children and with the teacher or care provider should be planned.

In addition, the program should provide planned child-centered activities from the time the child arrives at the child care setting until the child leaves it. The activities should enrich the child's experiences at home, at school, and in the community. The program should provide a balanced mix of group and individual activities.

The program should provide a rhythm during the day, with intervals of stimulation and relaxation, and a balance between periods of active play and quiet play or rest. It should have flexibility, as well as continuity, and should be related to the incremental developmental requirements of children involved.

- Regularity, through continuity and consistency, prepares children for what will happen next.
- Transitions between activities or classrooms should be made gradually and predictably. Necessary room or teacher shifts should be discussed with the children ahead of time to help them prepare for these changes.

• Stability and reliability is important to the positive development of children.

The program should offer the child opportunities to play outdoors every day, weather and climate permitting, with equipment that encourages exercise for physical development and the use of large muscles.

The program should offer the child opportunities to develop a sense of mastery and competence that comes from responding to the challenges of real tasks. Tasks and activities that promote independence from adults and encourage children to accept responsibility for their own behavior should be part of the program.

The program should recognize that experiences children have with their families are an important part of their lives and should be acknowledged; children must feel that their parents—and their parents' standards and values—are respected. In addition, the program should be aware of and sensitive to the different cultural backgrounds of the children it serves.

Developmentally Appropriate Learning Activities

1.5   Developmentally Appropriate Learning Activities

The daily activities in the child care program should be developmentally appropriate and designed to meet the individual needs of those children participating. Learning activities should include all areas of development with focus on cognitive (especially language development), social, emotional, physical, and character (moral) development (see Table 1).

1.6   Developmentally Appropriate Learning Activities for the Infant

The developmental program for infants (children ages birth to 12 months or children from birth to walking) in the child care service should include a daily schedule of stimulating activities; interaction with others, especially the care provider; and opportunities to actively explore and have new experiences in an environment structured to satisfy the children's needs. The

Table 1. Developmental Activities for Children in Child Care

	Infants (Birth–12 Months)*	Toddlers (1–3 years)*	Preschool (3–5 years)*	School-Age (5 and Older)*
Social/Emotional	-Consistent caregiver -Respect/involve parents -Respond promptly to needs -Positive physical handling (e.g. hugging, swaddling) -Supervision and play at all times	-Consistent caregiver -Respect/Involve parents -Encourage friendships among children -Respond promptly to needs -Positive physical handling (e.g. hugging, swaddling) -Supervision and play at all times	-Same as before -Guidance in dealing with problems -Guidance in talking about/understanding feelings	-Encourage/foster cooperation, social interaction -Allow for individualization -Adult role models -Appreciation/understanding of different cultures, etc. -Allow/encourage choice -Encourage identification with adults -Discuss problems
Language	-Regular use of language (talking, singing, etc.)	- Reading, storytelling -Identify objects with words -Opportunities for listening to/singing age-appropriate songs	-Reading, storytelling -Encourage conversation, communication to solve problems	-Provide space and time for homework
Physical	-Provide healthy, safe, clean environment (applies to all age groups) -Room to explore with safe borders and limits	-Manipulative toys available for fine motor skill development -Help with self-feeding, self-help skills -Provide space for jumping, running, etc., and equipment such as push/pull toys for coordination development	-Safe routines -Opportunities to explore -Opportunities to use toys and instruments such as pegboards or scissors -Opportunities for riding, climbing, swinging	-Occasions to explore outdoors -Opportunities for outdoor, active play -Physical space to challenge energy

The Quality Child Care Program   47

Cognitive	-Consistency and repetition of daily events with slight variations -Variation in environment with some limits	-Use puzzles, etc. for trial/error manipulations -Explore cause/effect -Use materials for sorting/classifying -Use sensory materials (water, sand) -Items available for exploration and curiosity stimulation	-Opportunities for dramatic play -Trips within the community -Exposure to many art forms -Stimulation to create stories -Opportunities to care for plants/animals -Freedom to use different media such as paint, clay, wood, etc.	-Choice in activities (provide space, opportunities for range of activities) -Exposure to creative materials
Character (Moral)	-Model appropriate interactions	-Model appropriate interactions, behaviors -Encourage understanding of right from wrong	-Tasks to help the group appropriate to age (setting table, etc.) -Help in making appropriate choices	-Opportunities for leadership, problem solving, decision making, and to take responsibility for actions and activities
Self-Help Skills	-Imitation and naming games encourage learning at an early age.	-Independent self-help skills are developed including self-feeding, cup-holding, chewing, taking off socks, unzipping large zippers, washing hands	-Tasks to learn responsibility (dressing, undressing, eating, drinking, toileting, oral/nasal hygiene)	-Encourage independence through preparing/serving snacks/meal

* Ages should be considered parameters/suggestions. Because children develop at different speeds and times, developmental activities should be based on child's developmental level/milestones more than on his or her specific age. See standards for milestone-based definitions.

daily program of the child care service should provide individualized, consistent, and continuous care from one primary care provider with whom the infant can interact.

Social/emotional

The social and emotional development of a child begins at birth. From birth to 12 months, children develop and change at a rapid pace. The developmental learning program of the child care program should work to promote positive development in this area.

- A consistent primary care provider should be assigned to each infant to enable the care provider to become familiar with that child's individual needs and cues, and to develop a daily schedule based on them. Care of each infant by a primary care provider helps the infant to establish rhythms in sleeping, crying, feeding, and elimination.

- Care providers should be responsive, affectionate, and accepting, so that the infant can develop the trust needed to become an autonomous person.

- The infant should receive positive physical contact through holding, cuddling, bathing, feeding, lifting, changing clothing, and other daily events. Care providers should promote an infant's sense of security by making him or her feel protected and meeting his or her needs when they arise.

- A positive and respectful relationship between parents and care providers can reduce the distress caused by strangers.

- Care providers should show appreciation toward the infant to make the infant feel that others see him or her as a worthwhile person, with a special identity and unique needs, while also a member of a family. The care providers should also assist infants to develop self-confidence and reinforce desirable behaviors.

Language/literacy

The first years of life are key in the development of cognitive and language abilities. The infant care program of the child care service should be based on infants' developmental needs. Because adult-child communication is important to the development of language and understanding in children, it should be a key part of the learning program.

- Language should be used to respond to sounds the infant makes by interpreting things verbally and through singing, talking, and reading at all times during the day and in all activities.

Cognitive

Routine tasks should be used for learning experiences. The environment should be used as a tool for learning by providing contrasts in colors, textures, and design.

- Daily events should be consistent and repetitive, with some varied and contrasting opportunities for experiences in new activities.
- Care providers should use toys, playthings, and other materials that stimulate development and learning.

Physical

To stimulate physical development, care providers should allow for moving about and playing in an expanding indoor and outdoor environment that is safe and supportive.

- Care providers should provide appropriate safe limits and perimeters for exploration.

Moral character

Adults should always model appropriate behavior and interactions for the infants in their care.

- Care providers should model acceptance of and exposure to people of diverse genders, ethnicity, and cultures.

Self-help skills

To encourage learning at an early age, care providers should provide opportunities for imitation and naming games.

1.7   Developmentally Appropriate Learning Activities for the Toddler

The developmental learning program for toddlers* in the child care service should provide, in a structured environ-

---

* Children 1 to 3 years of age or from walking to development of self-care skills such as using the toilet.

ment, activities in language development, cognitive skill development, fine motor skill development, and gross motor skill development.

Social/emotional

As with infants, it is important for toddlers to have a consistent, responsive care provider.

- Friendships and interpersonal relationships will begin to develop at this age and should be encouraged and cultivated.
- Toddlers should begin to learn how to problem solve for themselves and learn basic self-help skills such as dressing and feeding themselves.

Language/literacy

The basis for literacy comes from exposure to language and associated skills in the toddler years.

- The developmental learning program for toddlers should contain regular periods for storytelling and reading to the children.
- An attractive and comfortable area should be established for books and reading. Books should have bright, clear pictures and few words.
- Care providers should help children identify the words for common objects such as familiar toys, parts of the body, and so on.
- Care providers should provide auditory stimulation and create opportunities for learning and listening to age-appropriate children's songs and for playing instruments.

Cognitive

To promote cognitive skills development, the child care program should create appropriate activities and provide appropriate materials.

- The developmental learning program should create opportunities for trial and error manipulations, such as puzzles, pegboards, and connecting pieces.
- Opportunities should exist to explore cause and effect (e.g., repetitive activities of filling and emptying

objects, stacking and knocking down cups or blocks, hammering and pounding, and opening and closing).

- Materials should include sensory materials such as water and sand play, as well as materials for sorting and classifying.
- Age-appropriate technology and associated skills should be introduced to toddlers when they are ready.
- Items in nature should be made available for exploration and stimulation of concept development and curiosity.

Physical

The years after children initially learn to walk are important in their physical development for both fine and gross motor skills.

- The developmental learning program of the child care service should have manipulative toys available, such as snap-together or building blocks, for promoting small-muscle and eye-hand coordination.
- Care providers should offer support and encouragement in the development of self-feeding and other self-help skills.
- For gross motor skill development, the program should have adequate space for jumping, running, and climbing and equipment to encourage the development of coordination (e.g., push-pull toys, riding toys, or playground equipment).

Moral character

Care providers should model appropriate interactions and behaviors for toddlers to emulate.

- Toddlers should begin to gain an understanding of right from wrong, encouraged by explanations and demonstrations by the care providers.

Self-help skills

Care providers should create opportunities for developing independent self-help skills, including self-feeding, chewing, cup-holding, taking off socks, unzipping large zippers, and washing hands.

1.8 Developmentally Appropriate Learning Activities for the Preschool-Age Child

The developmental learning program for preschool-age children 3 to 5 years of age (or children who have achieved self-care practices up to entry in kindergarten) in the child care service should be planned so that each day offers opportunities to learn about themselves, others, and the world by observing, interacting, and seeking solutions to concrete problems.

Social/emotional

Preschool-age children should be given opportunities to learn how to identify, talk about, and understand feelings of pride, anger, grief, pleasure, and fear as they cope with new experiences and new relationships.

- Children should be encouraged to talk about these feelings and the feelings of others and given help in appropriately expressing strong emotions.
- Children should be encouraged to form friendships and develop socializing skills.
- Children should be offered help in cooperating, negotiating, and talking with others in all day-to-day activities and especially to solve interpersonal differences.
- Children should be allowed to make appropriate choices but be given help in facing these new challenges. The child care service should offer opportunities to absorb multicultural experiences (e.g., multicultural books, toys, props, etc.).

Cognitive and language/literacy

The developmental learning program for preschool-age children should offer exposure to new materials such as paint, clay, wood, cloth, and paper, and should give children the freedom to use these.

- Children should be exposed to many art forms to foster an appreciation for art.
- Children should have access to toys such as puzzles and instruments such as scissors and paintbrushes and these should be used on a regular basis in the preschool classroom.

- Children should be given opportunities to develop concepts of time, space, weight, distance, and measurement, and begin to use symbols.
- Children should be given opportunities to observe and be responsible for growing plants and to care for animals (e.g., a class pet).
- Children should be given opportunities for dramatic play and encouraged to create stories and poems from their own experiences, feelings, and imagination.

The goal for preschool-age children should always be school-readiness. Emphasis should be on the basic reading and writing skills (e.g., letter identification, proper spoken grammar, etc.) needed to succeed in kindergarten and beyond.

Physical

Preschool-age children should be able to explore their physical space freely. They should have ample opportunities for climbing, jumping, swinging, riding, running, galloping, skipping, balancing, and noncompetitive games.

Moral character

Preschool-age children should be given opportunities to perform tasks to help the group and learn responsibility, such as setting the table or cleaning up after a game.

- Care providers should help the preschool-age child to develop skills for making appropriate choices and decisions, and for gaining a positive sense of self and others, including such qualities as patience, empathy, tolerance, and forgiveness.

Self-help skills

Preschool-age children should be given tasks that assist them in becoming increasingly able to carry out daily self-care through dressing, undressing, eating, drinking, toileting, and oral and nasal hygiene.

1.9   Developmentally Appropriate Learning Activities for the School-Age Child

The developmental learning program for school-age children ages 5 to 12 in a child care service should allow for individualization, self-selection of activities, and recreation according to each child's needs and interests.

The developmental learning program for the school-age child should take into account variations of the school term.

- On school days, children will be in the child care program for fewer hours of care (before and after school).
- During school holidays and summer vacations, children will likely need a full-day program.

The developmental learning program for the school-age child should be designed differently based on the time of day and hours of care.

- Children should be offered quiet activities and a time to visit with their friends in the morning before school.
- Children should be offered opportunities for fresh air, exercise, and a broader choice of activities in the hours after school.
- Children in summer programs should be offered activities that require several days or weeks to complete, including time to explore the community and participate in specialized learning activities, such as swimming or other mini-courses.

The developmental learning program should always include activities and curriculum that foster cooperation and social interaction.

Social/emotional

The developmental learning program for the school-age child should be based on the child's level of maturity, ability to make decisions and accept responsibility, and range of interests; and the experiences and resources available in the school and community.

- Child care providers should recognize and encourage the increasing identification with adults by children of this age group, particularly if care for these children is provided in a facility that also provides a program for younger children.
- The developmental learning program should provide for the acceptance and nurturance of all children as

well as promote an appreciation for cultural and ethnic differences and acceptance of and respect for all
people.

School-age children are sometimes reluctant to continue to
attend the child care program once they have started school,
particularly if it separates them from the activities of their
school and neighborhood friends.

- Parents and care providers should plan together for
an appropriate variation in the child's program, so
that each child also may participate in other planned
group programs in the community.

- The child care service may use screened volunteers
to take children on special excursions or to escort
them to other community activities, using appropriate safety precautions.

Cognitive/language

The developmental learning program for school-age children should include activities to stimulate language development and cognitive thinking, including:

- access to creative materials, science and nature material, photography equipment, music, dance, stories,
poetry, and dramatic play;

- opportunities to explore and study their community
and to take trips, particularly during vacation periods, to museums, zoos, aquariums, factories, baker-
ies, etc.;

- opportunities to acquire skills in arts and crafts, to
learn organized games, and to learn to engage in soli-
tary activities; and

- opportunities for doing homework, tutoring, etc., to
enhance school performance.

Physical

The developmental learning program for school-age children should provide them with enough physical space to
channel their energy and should give them physical tasks
and activities to enhance physical fitness and promote a
healthy lifestyle.

Moral character

Children of school age are capable of considerable sympathetic understanding and, if they are helped, can gain insight and support from each other.

- The atmosphere of the child care program and the skills of the care providers should encourage children to discuss problems that arise in the program, or those they bring with them from school or home.
- Children should be given tasks and provided with adult role models that assist them in gaining a positive sense of self and others, including such qualities as leadership, patience, empathy, tolerance, and forgiveness.
- Children should be given the opportunity to take responsibility, consistent with their development and age, for planning activities and assisting in implementing such activities through, for example, participating on committees.

Self-help skills

Care providers should offer opportunities for school-age children to learn independence through such activities as preparing and serving foods, and taking care of and putting away materials.

Meeting the Needs of Children with Special Needs

1.10 Services for Children with Special Needs

The child care program serving children with special needs should modify its daily program, physical facilities, and materials to meet their developmental needs. The children should be placed in the environment that best suits their needs so they can be successful and the program should integrate the children into their regular program.

The child care program should have:

- a definition of the special needs for which it is prepared to give service, understanding that the program must comply with the requirements of the federal Americans with Disabilities Act, as well as any appropriate state and local requirements;

- an individual plan for each child with special needs;
- a program of developmentally appropriate services designed for each child's needs;
- a service implementation timetable for each child;
- a directory of available services and a mechanism for referral and follow-up;
- staff training to sharpen observation and techniques for appropriate interventions with various special-needs children;
- equipment and facility modifications adapted to the child's disability;
- mechanisms to help the child's parents access services to meet other needs of the child;
- access to consultation for the development of a multidisciplinary assessment and/or treatment plan; and
- a process of initial and continuous sharing of developmental health information among child care providers, parents, and primary health care providers.

The individualized plan for a child with special needs should specify the program requirements, specialized care, and facilities needed to further the child's participation in the child care program, as well as projected goals and objectives for participation. The child's goals should be based on the intent to normalize the child care experiences of the child. If the child's individualized plan is developed by the local school system or by another community agency, the staff of the child care program should be a participant in the plan's development and implementation.

1.11 Services for Children with Special Medical and Health-Related Needs

The child care program accepting children with special medical and health-related needs should be prepared to provide appropriate services.

Child care for children with special medical and health-related needs calls for appropriate staffing, both in number of staff members and in special training for work with the children being served.

To ensure the continuity so important for these children, a close working relationship between the parent, the child care service, and the community agencies or people involved in the child's medical care should be developed and sustained.

The Role of Parents in Quality Programming

1.12 Parent Involvement

The child care service should ensure that parents are involved in all decisions about the child care service program that affect their child, from enrollment through the termination of service.

If parents choose to use child care, they should have the right to decide whether center care, group family care, or a family care home is most appropriate for their child, and to select the particular program to use.

Parental involvement should be tailored to the parents' needs and culture. Parental involvement should reflect a partnership with parents and families and should be a continuous, ongoing process.

Information should be culturally appropriate and available in the language most commonly used by the parents.

1.13 Written Agreement of Responsibility

The child care service should ensure that parents (including parents, caregivers, guardians, and grandparents) have a clear understanding of the functions they are delegating to the child care service, including responsibility for the well-being and safety of their children while those children are in the child care program. This understanding should be recorded in a written agreement in the language commonly used by the parents and signed both by the parents (or legal guardians) and by a representative of the child care service.

This agreement should include:

- recognition that parents retain their legal rights and responsibilities for their children, even though they voluntarily agree to share care of their children with the child care service;

- recognition that parents and the child care service are voluntarily entering into a partnership to provide care for the child;

- authorization to obtain emergency medical care if the child becomes ill or has an injury while attending the child care program and the parents cannot be reached immediately (see 2.12); and

- delineation of the mutual responsibilities of the parents and child care staff to support the child.

1.14 Role of Staff Members in Supporting Parents

Each staff member of the child care service should be responsible for facilitating communication between parents and the program and building mutual understanding and respect.

Parents may need help to better understand their vital role in the child care experience of their child. Parents and child care staff members should engage in an ongoing exchange of information on all important matters affecting the child.

Parents should expect to receive support from all staff members, as well as an understanding of the important role parents play in the partnership. As a representative of the child care service, each staff member should act with the goals of the service in mind. Parents may also find support in a special relationship with a particular staff member.

1.15 Participation of Parents at Enrollment

When parents apply for a child care program, the child care service should give them the opportunity to discuss with the service staff member responsible for enrollment whether the program will meet their needs and the needs of their child. The parents and the staff member should also discuss how the proposed service is provided and what procedures they should follow to help the child obtain the full benefit of the child care experience.

The enrollment interview should set the tone for the partnership among the parents, the child care service, and the staff members.

1.16 Parents' Roles in Preparing Their Child for Beginning the Child Care Experience and for Changing Child Care Programs

The child care service should encourage parents to prepare their child for the new experiences of initial placement, any movements to new groups within a service, or movement to new services/agencies.

When children are moved from a group because of behavioral problems, both parents and children need to understand the experience as a move to a more appropriate setting rather than a termination or failure.

1.17 Parents' Roles in Developing Individual Child Plans

The child care service should ensure that parents are directly involved with staff members in determining their child's individual child care plan.

Daily communication between staff members and parents about the child's progress or problems will facilitate this joint effort. If significant differences in perspectives or goals persist, parents and staff members should have access to supervisory and consultation services.

1.18 Individual Conferences with Parents During the Child Care Experience

The child care service should schedule periodic individual conferences between child care staff members and parents in addition to the daily informal contacts.

Conferences should be used to discuss the child's progress toward the planned objectives and any need to modify them.

The roles of both the child care service and the parents should be reviewed during the conference to assure that each is carrying out the defined responsibilities detailed in the plan.

Parents should be continually informed about their child's experiences in the program so they can relate those experiences to the child's experiences at home and in school.

1.19 Supporting Parents

The child care service should ensure that parents are able to obtain the support they need to help them use the child care service effectively, and to cope with the stresses they face related to the rearing and development of their children.

The child care service may offer:

- support for cultural and diversity issues facing parents,
- networking in peer support groups,
- parenting and child development education,
- activities to model parenting skills,
- counseling,
- referral to community and public agencies for assistance, and
- legislative and funding information.

1.20 Parent Group Meetings

The child care service should schedule parent group meetings several times a year for education and mutual support.

The needs and interests of the families involved should determine the number of meetings and their timing, purpose, and agenda.

- Meetings may be held as social gatherings, for parent education, or for discussion of common problems or concerns.
- For some parents, small discussion groups with a trained leader are of greater benefit then individual sessions because many parents receive reassurance from seeing that other parents share their concerns.

Staff members should be expected to participate in parent-group meetings as appropriate, so that parents and staff members become better acquainted and have a different setting in which to develop their partnership.

When planning meetings, planners should keep in mind that regular scheduling of meetings establishes continuity for long-term discussions.

Planning of meetings is best achieved through coordinated efforts of staff members and parent representatives.

2

The Health, Safety, and Nutrition Program

Goals

    I. The health, safety, and nutrition of the children are paramount and integral components of the child care program.

    II. The child care program helps parents obtain qualified health and mental health services for their children.

    III. The child care service ensures that the facility is structurally sound, free from fire hazards, and maintained in a sanitary condition.

    IV. The child care program provides nutritional meals to the children and offers nutrition information to the parents.

Concern for health, safety, and nutrition, and an understanding of the relationship of the physical, emotional, and intellectual growth processes of the child, should be reflected in all aspects of the child care service and translated into the daily experiences of the children served.

Each member of the center staff and each family and group home child care provider should contribute to the promotion of good health for children. Each member of the staff should be informed of the health and nutrition recommendations for each child, understand his or her role in implementing them, and be current on the community's available health care resources. Effective communication among staff members facilitates sharing observations and planning common goals.

2.1   Responsibility for the Health Care* of Children in the Child Care Service

The child care service should be prepared to help parents obtain primary health care for their children if such assistance is needed, recognizing, however, that parents should be responsible for the ongoing health care of their children.

Parents should be expected to use their family physician (pediatrician, general practitioner, or family practitioner) for their child's health supervision and medical treatment. Community resources available to all parents, such as a child health clinic or a hospital outpatient department, can also provide primary health care and supervision.

The child care service should support parents by recognizing their primary role in assuring appropriate health care for their children. The child care service, however, should help parents, if necessary, obtain medical, psychological, dental, visual, and hearing evaluations, in addition to any remedial care necessary to address those conditions that could interfere with the child's proper growth and development.

Children with special needs may require special health care services.

2.2   Administering the Responsibilities for Health Care Services with the Child Care Service

The child care service should have a health policy that protects, maintains, and promotes the health of the children in its

---

*   In this volume, *health care* includes the provision of primary and specialty care, preventive care, illness prevention, and health promotion. It implies availability and access to medical care (insurance). Areas covered include nutrition, oral health, child development, mental health, provision of adaptive equipment, and medications.

care, and should have a single focal point for its health care services. It should retain the services of a health care consultant or work in conjunction with the local department of health to develop policies for preventive and safety services and for handling any injury or illness and to support parents in the supervision of their children's health concerns. Another consultant, such as a nurse, should be available to help providers understand the health needs of individual children and the management of communicable diseases.

Child care providers should integrate the health, safety, and nutritional programs with the other aspects of the service. They should define the duties of the health care consultants and assure that recommendations from them are properly carried out.

The child care service may create a health advisory committee, to include parents and individuals with expertise in the various child health disciplines, to advise on health care needs and interests.

The child care program should orient its health care supervision toward the promotion of good health as well as protection from disease.

Assessing Health Care Needs

2.3   Initial Health Evaluation

The child care program should ensure that all children have an initial health evaluation before entering the child care service.

The initial evaluation should identify any health problems that might require attention. It should be performed as a protection for the child, other children, and staff members with whom the child may come in contact.

The initial health evaluation should be made by health care professionals knowledgeable about child health and development, and about child care. These may include a physician qualified in child health, a nurse practitioner, or a physician's assistant under the supervision of a physician.

The evaluation should be conducted in the least intrusive environment for the child.

The child care service may want to maintain a list of such professionals for parents who are enrolling their children.

2.4   Components of the Health Evaluation

The child care service should ensure that the initial health evaluation for the child entering the program includes a developmental and health history and assessment, a complete physical examination, a report of immunizations, a screening for hearing and vision problems, and a mental health screening when appropriate or necessary.

> Where appropriate, *Caring for Our Children: National Health and Safety Performance Standards* (U.S. DHHS, Maternal and Child Health Bureau, 2002) should be consulted.*

2.5   Health Records

The child care service should maintain a comprehensive health record for each child, including a record of immunizations, illnesses, emergency contact information, and the findings and recommendations of all physical examinations.

> When the child leaves the child care service, a copy of the health record should be turned over to the parents, or, with their permission, to the family physician.

> In accordance with the Health Insurance Portability and Accountability Act (HIPAA, P.L. 104-191) of 1996, no information concerning a child's health or mental health should be released to anyone without permission from the child's parents or guardians. Child care providers should not release any information to any outsiders regarding the health or mental health of any of the children in their care.

2.6   Obtaining Health and Mental Health History Records

The child care service should obtain the record of relevant health and mental health history information from medical,

---

* Published by the American Academy of Pediatrics, American Public Health Association, and National Resource Center for Health and Safety in Child Care.

mental health, and developmental learning personnel, from the family, and from social service sources when circumstances, such as signs of child abuse or neglect or serious behavior problems, indicate a need for this additional information.

Necessary health and mental health information should be obtained from the parents whenever possible, as well as from previous care providers identified by the child's parents. It should, at a minimum, include any vulnerabilities of the child, such as:

- a description of health habits and behavior, including sleeping habits and toilet training issues and successful approaches to challenging behaviors;
- a history of communicable diseases, accidents, and hospitalizations;
- perinatal and newborn records;
- dental and orthodontic records;
- current and chronic illnesses and limitations;
- current medications;
- allergies or dietary restrictions;
- recent exposures to communicable diseases;
- immunization records;
- special equipment needs, such as orthopedic shoes or glasses;
- the names and contact information for health and mental health providers; and
- results of testing and comprehensive assessment and treatment and support recommendations.

2.7   Releases for Health, Mental Health, and Developmental Learning Information

From the child's parents or legal guardians, the child care service should obtain written releases for additional health, mental health, and developmental learning information about the child, when the circumstances call for such additional information. Three-way consent forms that include the child care service, parents, and primary health provider are recommended.

2.8   Promotion of Health

The child care service should orient the health supervision of the children toward the promotion of good physical and mental health, as well as protection from disease.

The child care service should offer parents opportunities to learn about the safety and health needs of their children, such as nutrition, exercise, the prevention of accidents, the relationship of foods and nutrition to health and development, and the importance of good food habits and attitudes (see Chapter 1).

The daily activities of the child care service should promote positive health attitudes, habits, and personal hygiene by means of examples, routines, and age-appropriate discussions.

2.9   Observation of the Health of Children

Staff members and providers in the child care service who are in daily contact with children should observe the children's overall health and make note of any health concerns. Such daily observation should supplement routine health examinations and should be considered in evaluating the health status of every child in care.

Providers should bring to the attention of parents and, when necessary, the health care consultant, their observations of behaviors or conditions that might be an indication of a child's need for an evaluation by a health care provider.

The observation of children should also include attention to possible signs of physical abuse, neglect, or substance abuse. Care providers' observations of changes in appearance or behavior over a period of time should be discussed with parents, and if necessary, with the health care consultant.

2.10 Daily Medical Care

Children in the child care service requiring medication during the day, variations in diet, or special medical procedures should receive them in the child care facility only on the written order of a physician, in accordance with state law.

Special medical procedures for an individual child should be the responsibility of a physician or of health department personnel coming to the child care facility.

Medications (prescription or nonprescription) should be given to a child only with written permission, including administration procedures, from the parents or guardians and the child's physician.

All medications should be carefully labeled with the child's name. Medications should be kept in their original containers together with all other pertinent information, including directions for use and storage, date filled, and physician's name for prescription medications.

A record of medication administered (dosage and time) should be included in the child's health records.

Medications should be stored as directed by their labels, kept out of the reach of children, and returned to the parents or discarded when no longer needed.

2.11 Access to Health Services

The child care service should be prepared to help parents obtain qualified health and mental health services for their children.

Methods for assisting parents may include:

- providing parents with a list of community and public agencies (with contact numbers) that can help the family to obtain an appropriate primary health provider and other providers, as needed (e.g., physical therapy, home health services, public health services, access to mobile screening units); and

- advocating for qualified physicians, dentists, mental health personnel, and other providers willing and able to work with children in child care.

  - Local chapters of pediatric societies and family practitioners may join with the child care staff to educate private medical providers regarding the health care needs of children in child care and the processes to be used in becoming a service provider for these children.

2.12 Emergency Medical Care

The child care service should have access to emergency medical care available to all children in its care.

The child care service should develop policies and procedures to assure that necessary consents are obtained from parents at the time of enrollment (see 1.13) and that staff are trained to respond in a helpful and timely manner to emergency situations.

2.13 Staff Wellness Issues

All child care service staff members in child care centers or family child care providers should undergo a comprehensive physical examination prior to employment and at least every two years during their employment.

All staff should receive TB (tuberculosis) screening tests prior to employment and once a year when required by the local or state health department.

The center or home should have all staff medical examination records (e.g., immunization records, review of risk of exposure, etc.) on file and should follow the same procedures for confidentiality as are followed with the children's records.

Administrators should assess staff members' health on a daily basis through observation. When staff members are ill, they should follow the same guidelines for being absent as the children in their care. The administration is responsible for finding a substitute and should not allow ill staff members to remain at work.

2.14 Smoking

The child care service should require that centers and family or group child care homes be smoke free.

2.15 Sleep Environment

Every facility in the child care service should provide a place and a time for rest periods/naps for infants, toddlers, and preschool-age children.

Infants should be placed on their back for sleeping to lower the risk of SIDS (Sudden Infant Death Syndrome) unless a physician provides directions for another sleeping position.

Gas-trapping objects such as pillows or quilts should not be placed under or with the infant while sleeping.

If infants can roll into different positions, they should be placed on their backs but allowed to move to whatever position they prefer for sleep.

The nap area should be set up to reduce distractions and allow for quiet. All children should have access to the nap area whenever they desire or need a rest. There should be individualized cribs and cots, as developmentally appropriate, with space between sleeping areas.

2.16 Control of Communicable Disease

The child care service should develop a set of written health and safety policies and precautions for preventing and controlling the spread of communicable diseases among the children in its care and their families.

The following policies and procedures should be put into effect:

- The child care service should require proof of age-appropriate immunization against diptheria, pertussis (whooping cough), hepatitis B, tetanus, varicella (chicken pox), poliomyelitis, measles, rubella (German measles), and mumps in accordance with the most recent periodicity schedule of the American Academy of Pediatrics (released every January). Infants who are too young to be immunized at the time of admission should be immunized at the appropriate time or sooner if there is a potential community epidemic.

- The child care provider should observe all children daily for signs of illness.

- Children who show obvious signs of illness (e.g., their behavior is affected, they are unable to participate in regular activities) should be separated from the group and placed in a separate quiet area under adult supervision. A determination, in consultation with the parents, should be made as to whether or how quickly the child should be removed for more appropriate care or treatment.

- The best place for ill children is at home with a parent. If this is not possible, the child care service may care for mildly ill children as long as staff supervision is available and all children are adequately cared for, as consistent with state regulations.

- Under no circumstances should the child care service care for seriously ill children or admit obviously ill children to its program.

- The child care service may have a get-well room that is licensed to provide care for children who are mildly ill. Guidance for the care of mildly ill children is provided in *Caring for Our Children: National Health and Safety Performance Standards*, Standards 3.070–3.080 (U.S. DHHS, Maternal and Child Health Bureau, 2002).

- Parents of all children in child care should be advised to seek medical care if the child appears ill or has an injury, and should be helped to obtain it and/ or referred to health care resources, if useful.

- Children absent for illness should be checked by a physician, when indicated, before they return to the child care program. Family child care homes may exercise greater flexibility if there is no risk to other children.

- Whenever exposure to communicable disease has occurred in a group of children, the health care profession should be consulted about proper instructions to give parents of exposed children and about the propriety of control measures. The local public health officer or a health consultant may also be called on for expertise in the management of communicable diseases. A written policy should set forth the program's response to known exposure to or infection with contagious diseases in the child care setting (e.g., chicken pox, strep throat).

- The local public health department should be consulted about regulations during epidemics, such as restrictions on admission of children not already exposed to the disease. The temporary closing of the child care facility may be indicated in certain situations.

- Children with a contagious condition such as impetigo, scabies, or pediculosis should be excluded from contact with others until the condition is brought under control; if needed, a physician or public health nurse should address the situation and determine if it is safe for the child to return to the home or center.

- All staff members of the child care service, including family child care and group family care providers, teachers, assistants, maintenance personnel, cooks, and volunteers, should have preemployment and subsequent biennial examinations, tuberculin tests, and if indicated, chest x-rays.

To improve the child's resistance to disease and to prevent exposure to disease, the child care service should:

- encourage/support breast feeding and the use of breast milk for age-appropriate children;

- provide food that contributes to the child's daily nutritional needs;

- store and prepare food under sanitary conditions to avoid contamination, food-borne infections, and diseases;

- protect children from overheating or chilling;

- wet mop and dust rooms with appropriate antiviral and antibacterial agents when children are not present; and

- avoid overcrowding children or exposing them to others not under the same type of medical control.

2.17 Policy and Procedures on HIV/AIDS, Body Fluid Transmission, and Blood-Borne Diseases

The child care service should have a written policy in place that specifies how the program will serve or accommodate children and staff members who may be infected with HIV. All parents, staff members, and funding sources must be informed of the policy. It should reflect those issues a provider will be dealing with in the day-to-day operation of the child care program.

The child care service provider should be aware that they might be unknowingly serving children who are infected with HIV. Not all children who are infected have been diagnosed, and some children who are infected have no visible symptoms.

The provider should consult federal, state, and local laws and regulations protecting disabled individuals, including laws and regulations that mandate that individuals are not to be discriminated against on the basis of their disability (Americans with Disabilities Act).

The policy statement should include sections on personnel issues, enrollment, infection control, testing, and confidentiality.

Personnel issues and rights of staff members

Federal law mandates that no one should be denied employment, the continuation of employment, or the right to volunteer at a facility solely on the basis of HIV status.

Mandatory HIV testing of potential employees or volunteers should not be required.

In addition, the facility should maintain confidentiality of information about staff members or volunteers who are known to be HIV positive.

Because HIV is not transmitted through casual interaction, request for transfers to avoid contact with coworkers with HIV infection or AIDS should be denied on the grounds that the risk of contagion is not a valid factor.

Enrollment

No child should be excluded from the child care service solely on the basis of his or her HIV status.

The parents or guardians and the staff member in charge of enrollment should conduct a customary review of the appropriateness of the service, the ability of the staff and facility to provide appropriate care, and the ability of the child to benefit from the program, as would be done for any child.

Enrollment of a child should always be in response to the child's needs and the program's ability to meet them.

With the consent of the parent or guardian, the child's physician may provide information regarding the child's HIV status at intake.

Infection control

Although only infected blood, semen, or vaginal fluid transmit HIV, it is critical to focus generally on the importance of maintaining a clean and healthy child care environment.

Routine infection control (e.g., washing, measures taken to stay clean and healthy) should be used to decrease the spread of all infectious diseases. In addition, using, universal precautions, including taking steps to prevent contact with blood or bodily fluids, will help prevent the spread of blood-borne infections (HIV, hepatitis, etc.).

Testing for HIV infection

Decisions about testing a child for HIV infection should be made only by the child's parent and physician.

Mandatory testing is neither warranted nor recommended. Nevertheless, any unexplained medical or developmental changes should be brought to the attention of the parents.

In the case of adolescents, local laws about informed consent should be consulted.

Confidentiality

The policies of the child care service should contain a strong statement affirming the importance of confidentiality and a clear definition of need-to-know.

Information regarding the child who is HIV infected should be shared only with persons who are directly accountable for the child and those who have a need to know to meet the child's individual needs. Any communication between the child care provider and anyone outside the agency concerning the HIV status of a child should require the consent of the parent or guardian.

Children who are HIV infected need child care, if not in a regular child care setting, then in a setting designed for special care for HIV-infected children or infants. The decision about which setting best meets their needs should be made on a case-by-case basis, depending in part on the stage of the disease.

Safety

2.18 Safety and Risk Management

The child care service should implement a safety and risk-management program to prevent and reduce injury to its clients and personnel, minimize liability, and protect and preserve its assets.

The child care service should establish preventive policies and procedures to minimize the risk of negligent or willful misconduct of employees, theft and fraud, conflicts of interest, and physical injury to clients, staff members, and volunteers.

The safety and risk management process should include the establishment of written policies and procedures to both manage and reduce the liabilities to which the organization may be subject. Such policies and procedures should include, but not be limited to, the following:

- fire prevention and fire safety;
- disaster response;
- emergency plans, including evacuation plans;
- universal precautions;
- handling suspicious or hazardous materials;
- security;
- vehicle and driver safety;
- an on-call, chain-of-command response system that is well communicated, accessible, and posted in critical locations, including the staff office; and
- a process for formal reviewing accidents, illnesses, grievances, etc.

In addition to the above policies and procedures, the child care service should ensure that the facility is properly equipped to prevent safety problems or physical hazards and to respond to unsafe events or conditions. Measures may include but are not limited to:

- posting of evacuation routes at all egress locations;
- requiring all visitors to sign in and out when entering or leaving the facility; and
- adequate lighting on the grounds,

The child care service should meet all safety requirements of the relevant licensing and accrediting bodies. It also should provide training for all staff at hiring, and yearly thereafter to assure staff competency in all safety and risk procedures and to update staff on new procedures.

The child care service should provide opportunities for staff, children, and others on premises to practice the safety and risk procedures on a regular basis, documenting each practice event and any problems noted.

In addition, staff should be observed as they carry out safety and risk procedures, their performance evaluated, and any needed corrective measures or additional skill development addressed in a timely manner.

The child care service should create other ongoing mechanisms for ensuring safety, such as a cross-agency safety committee that meets regularly to review safety concerns, conduct safety inspections, and make recommendations to management regarding improvements.

2.19 Critical Incidents and Crisis Management

The child care service should have a structured process and policy in place to respond to and review child and staff-related critical incidents.

Critical incidents include, but are not limited to, the serious injury or death of a child receiving services, the unexplained absence of a child receiving services, and threats or acts of violence to staff providing child care services. Such incidents can suddenly compromise the safety of children in care, the routine functioning of staff, and the regular operations of the child care service.

Because they often are unanticipated and potentially life threatening, critical incidents, whether they be child- or staff-related incidents, have a tendency to create confusion, anxiety, and chaos when they occur. In the absence of a prompt yet methodical response, critical incidents can escalate in severity and endangerment. Therefore, written policies and procedures should be developed to:

   • identify the list of concrete tasks to be completed by those involved;

- delineate the expectations of staff and the chain of command;
- improve communication within the child care service;
- respond proactively as opposed to reactively;
- lessen the anxiety inherent in these situations; and
- increase direction, guidance, and support.

To provide adequate guidance on critical incidents, protocols and procedures should address:

- definitions and examples of critical incidents;
- notification processes—intra-agency, interagency (specifically, formal contact with law enforcement), and community, and public disclosure;
- crisis coverage—staff composition and function in the wake of the critical incident;
- fact-finding processes, which may vary depending on the nature of the critical incident;
- risk management procedures;
- policies regarding administrative leave;
- policies regarding media inquiries; and
- counseling and supportive services for affected parties.

Reviews of the critical incidents should focus on the actions of all parties involved with the affected child or staff. The review should:

- assess the actions and events that surround the critical incident,
- detail the individual and agency factors that may have contributed to the incident,
- determine what individual and agency factors should be addressed to reduce the likelihood of comparable critical incidents in the future, and
- result in an amendment to the written policies and procedures to reflect the changes indicated in the review process.

Although the focus of the critical incident review will vary depending on the nature of the incident and the specific expectations of the child care service and the involved community, the review should:

- use a multidisciplinary approach that includes representatives from the community agencies and organizations involved in protecting and serving children and their families;
- involve professionals who have been involved with the child and his/her family (when the critical incident is a child-related incident) as well as community members;
- respect the privacy and reputation of all involved parties and adhere to statutory provisions related to confidentiality and immunity;
- document findings of case-specific analyses to identify strategies in which the child care service and the provider community can better protect children and support families; and
- inform and educate the public, to the extent permissible, to increase understanding of and support for the needs of children who are receiving child care services.

2.20 Injuries and Illnesses

All staff members of the child care service who work directly with children should have a basic knowledge of first-aid principles and be regularly retrained every other year. At least one staff member trained in cardiopulmonary resuscitation (CPR) should be available to all children in the program at all times.

All child care facilities should have immediately available:

- a working telephone;
- a manual of first-aid procedures;
- first-aid kit in each classroom or home; and
- emergency telephone numbers for reaching parents, police, fire, and emergency medical services.

Every child's health care record should include all family and identified emergency contact telephone numbers, as well as the name of a primary health care provider to call or the name of the clinic or community outpatient hospital the family uses in emergencies. The child care service's own physician, health care consultant or local emergency room should be used if the child's physician cannot be reached.

2.21 Emergency and Disaster Procedures

The child care service should have in place clear instructions and plans for dealing with emergency situations, including those of disaster proportions (e.g., fire, flood, earthquake, hurricane, tornado, etc.).

Emergency plans should include clear instructions for contacting parents and guardians or next of kin in emergency situations.

All staff members should be trained in the emergency procedures (e.g., when to evacuate and when to remain in the building) and made aware of other community resources for disasters/emergencies. In family care homes, the training should include all adults living in the home or participating in the program there.

The child care service should send to all parents of children in care a written description of the child care service's emergency procedures. Parents should be consulted with respect to individual emergency care plans for their children. Prior written authorization allowing for the securing of emergency medical care in the absence of the parents should be obtained from the parents or guardians of each child in care.

2.22 General Injury or Illness Procedures

The child care service should always notify parents immediately when their child has had an injury or illness. A written factual record of each accident should be prepared and given to the parents.

If the parents cannot be reached, an emergency contact person designated by the parents should be notified.

The name and telephone number of the family's designated physician and date of child's last tetanus vaccine should be maintained by the child care service.

In addition, the child care service should have arrangements in place with a nearby hospital emergency room or health care facility to accept children from the child care service in the event of an emergency when the family physician cannot be reached promptly.

2.23 Evacuation Procedures

For each center and child care home under its auspices, the child care service should develop evacuation plans approved by a fire department inspector. Plans should include exits to be used, a statement of how children are to be familiarized with the procedures, and a schedule of evacuation drills for the year.

Each child care center or home should conduct monthly fire drills. A written record of evacuation drills should be maintained by the facility.

The evacuation plan should be prominently displayed in each room of the facility.

2.24 Structural Safety of Facilities

The child care service should make sure that children for whom it is responsible are cared for in a building (child care center or child care home) that is structurally sound, free from fire hazards, and maintained in a sanitary condition.

2.25 Prevention and Identification of Institutional Child Abuse

The child care service should develop policies for the prevention and identification of child abuse or neglect. Those policies should reflect the policies and procedures described in CWLA's *Standards of Excellence for Services to Abused or Neglected Children and Their Families* (1999).

The policies should include:

- guaranteeing the custodial parent open access to the program at all times;
- ensuring confidentiality of reporting in accordance with state law;

- standardized job screening, interviewing, and selection techniques to prevent the hiring of past child abuse/neglect offenders;
- background clearances on all applicants selected for employment, including obtaining those clearances required by the licensing agency;
- procedures for identifying and reporting all alleged incidents of abuse and neglect;
- staff training in identification and reporting procedures;
- guidelines on developmentally appropriate discipline in the child care setting (see 5.12);
- information for parents about child abuse prevention, reporting, and associated child protection policies; and
- education of children about reporting incidents of abuse or neglect to trusted adults.

The child care service should take steps to protect both children and staff members by maintaining required child-staff ratios and designing centers or homes to permit a clear view of all areas frequented by children so staff can observe everyone's behavior at all times.

2.26 Substance Abuse and Child Abuse

The child care service should be prepared to provide educational, preventative, and referral services to substance-abusing families.

The child care service provider has the opportunity to have daily, voluntary, informal contact with the parents of the children in child care.

CWLA member agencies providing child care services indicate a large number of the families they serve are involved with some form of substance abuse.

- Child care providers increasingly describe parents for whom addiction takes precedence over their children's safety, and families so dysfunctional that it is exceedingly difficult to work with them in the context of the child care service.

- Teachers/care providers are also experiencing threats to their own physical safety and are confronted with liability issues that compel them to become enforcers of rules rather than nurturers of children.

The child care service should have in its policies a clear statement of the child care service's practice of providing or summoning assistance should the person designated to pick up a child appear to be under the influence of alcohol or other drugs. People to whom the child may be released must be designated in writing. These policies should be clearly communicated to the parent at the time of enrollment, and the parents should be given a written copy and should attest to their receipt of the policy in writing.

All staff should be trained in identifying the signs of substance abuse so that they can take advantage of their daily contact with parents and identify problems before they lead to problems for the child.

All staff members should be fully briefed and updated as legal or insurance policy changed dictate on all requirements for child abuse and neglect reporting, including any required follow-up measures.

Although demand may increase for child care services to assist families (including foster and adoptive families) by providing crisis care, respite care, care for drug-exposed or drug-involved infants and children, or therapeutic child care for special-needs children, the child care service should first evaluate its resources for the training and support of the staff members required to adequately serve these growing populations.

2.27 Shaken Baby Syndrome

Teachers/care providers and parents should be aware of the symptoms of shaken baby syndrome and how to identify them. As with other forms of child abuse, child care staff and care providers should follow state and local reporting procedures when shaken baby syndrome is suspected.

Shaken baby syndrome is a term used to describe a variety of symptoms and problems that can arise in infants and young children when they have been shaken violently or hit in the head. Symptoms, mostly neurological, range from lethargy to retinal damage to seizure and even death.

Nutrition and Fitness

2.28 Preparation of Meals

The child care service should plan meals and snacks in the child care program in relation to the 24-hour needs of the child and should provide an appropriate proportion of the child's total daily requirements.

Menus, food preparation facilities, and food service procedures should be planned in consultation with a nutritionist and with a staff member from the local health department, in accordance with U.S. Department of Agriculture Child Care Food Program guidelines (1996).

The food served by the child care service should meet federal Food and Nutrition Service Guidelines for the Child Care Food Program. It should be nutritional, as recommended by the American Dietetic Association's nutritional standards for child care programs (1999), balanced for texture and taste, and attractively served.

When serving infant formula, the child care service should follow the appropriate storage, preparation, and feeding procedures in *Caring for Our Children: National Health and Safety Performance Standards*, Standards 4.013-4.020 (U.S. DHHS, Maternal and Child Health Bureau, 2002).

Menus should be posted daily or otherwise made available to parents. The child care service nutrition consultant should review food service plans, including plans to meet the special dietary needs of the children, as required.

Parents and child care staff should exchange information on menu planning and food habits, including food allergies and preferences.

Administration of any dietary supplement requires a physician's prescription. Additionally, individualizing the menu to meet a particular child's needs should be done only under a physician's direction.

Attention should be given to food customs and preferences of different ethnic groups represented in the child care service population. Cultural food preferences should be accommodated whenever possible and consistent with nutritional guidelines.

The atmosphere at mealtime should be comfortable and free from tensions or pressure.

Children should be encouraged to try unfamiliar foods, although individual food preferences should be recognized and food should never be used as means of discipline.

Children should neither be rewarded for eating nor punished for not eating.

Staff members should participate in the meal experience with the children. Children should be encouraged in a nonjudgmental manner to develop good eating habits and proper table manners.

2.29 Food Brought from Home

If the parent or legal guardian decides to provide meals for the child, the child care service should require a written agreement between the parent and the staff regarding the food brought to the facility.

The following requirements: should be applied to food provided by the parent or guardian:

- the food is labeled with child's name, the date, and the type of food;
- the food is not to be shared with other children; and
- all foods are properly refrigerated and protected against contamination.

The child care service should provide parents who wish to bring food from home with written nutritional guidelines established to meet the needs of the child.

The child care service should have supplemental food to provide to the child if food from home does not meet his or her nutritional needs.

If food from home consistently does not meet the nutritional needs of the child, the child care service should refer the parent to a nutrition specialist and provide food for the child.

2.30 Fitness and Exercise

The child care service should encourage and allow for daily physical activity to help develop and maintain the physical fitness of the children in its care.

Child care staff members should model healthy behaviors and teach children about the importance of regular physical activity.

2.31 Parent Education About Nutrition and Exercise

In addition to educating the children in their care about the importance of nutrition and exercise to proper development, the child care service should give parents, through regular health education programs or newsletters, culturally competent information about what their children need to develop to their potential.

The child care service should have a clear parent-education plan that details what resources they will use to educate the parents in addition to how they will disseminate information.

3

The Physical Environment

Goals

I. The child care service seeks advice and approval from zoning authorities, health and safety officials, regulatory agencies, and building inspectors (as appropriate) before proceeding with building plans and renovations.

II. The child care facility is accessible to children and families with physical disabilities.

III. The child care facility is designed and planned with consideration of the needs of the child care population to be served.

IV. The child care environment is clean, safe, properly equipped, and well maintained.

V. The child care facility has sufficient indoor and outdoor play space to accommodate children and staff comfortably.

VI. The child care service establishes systems for inspection and maintenance that ensure facilities and equipment are safe and well maintained.

The physical facilities used for child care should be regarded as a community resource for promoting the well-being of children and their families. Careful planning in selecting the site, the building type, the equipment, and the furnishings of the child care center is necessary to enable the program to achieve its objectives.

The buildings and equipment used for family or group child care homes should accommodate the needs of the children and families served by them. Consideration should be given to the ages, special needs, and other characteristics of the children to be served so that appropriate facilities are provided for the education, health, and social development of all children in the care of the child care service. The physical environment should reflect the cultural diversity of the children and families served by the program.

Planning or Building the Child Care Center

3.1   Building Plans

When undertaking any building program, the child care service should determine the allocation for the project, consider the perspectives of those to be served as well as others involved, and seek regulatory review of the proposed plans.

The governing body should determine the allocation available for the project and commission an architect of recognized standing to design and plan the project within the budgetary limit.

In preparing the building plan, consideration should be given to the perspectives of the families served, the governing body, management, child care staff, and all professionals who will provide services in the facility, including food service staff, child care staff, support staff, social workers, health consultants, volunteers, and maintenance staff.

Regulatory agencies should be asked to review and advise on proposed plans. Local zoning and building officers, as well as the fire and health departments, can help during the early stages of building or renovation to assure that plans conform to building codes and other special requirements.

3.2   Building Design

The child care service should ensure that buildings, whether new or renovated, are designed to serve the purposes of the child care program. There should be ample space and facilities to accommodate the number of children served and the personnel needed to maintain staffing patterns.

Such elements as the age of the children, services to be provided, and physical disabilities of the population to be served (e.g., wheelchair users, the visually impaired) should be considered in determining variations in space requirements, interior and exterior design, and the arrangement of rooms and equipment.

The following considerations should apply to the planning or refurbishing of a building to serve as a child care center:

- Buildings should be well constructed, durable, attractive, safe, secure, and functional in design.
- The building plan should provide for comfort, convenience, and easy maintenance, as well as maximum ease for staff members to fulfill the responsibility of supervising children both inside and outside the building.
- One-story buildings facilitate supervision, serve all age groups, reduce fire hazards, and eliminate stair climbing.
- The facility should provide access for people with physical disabilities and should be compliant with all applicable access regulations.
- All facilities should comply with or exceed appropriate fire, construction, and other safety codes.

3.3   Physical Access

The child care service should make its buildings and facilities accessible to its defined service population in compliance with applicable laws, regulations, and standards.

All new buildings, including entrances and emergency exits, floors, hallways, doorways and doors, furnishings, equipment and controls, water fountains, bathrooms, and telephones, should be made fully accessible to people with disabilities.

The child care service should ensure that the facility has an entry area where children can be dropped off and picked up easily and safely. If a child care center is in a multifunction building, it should have its own separate entrance.

The child care service should examine its existing buildings to determine the need for changes to provide access for children, families, staff, and visitors who have physical disabilities.

When the facility's age or excessive cost prohibit compliance of the entire building or all facilities, the child care service should ensure equal alternative access by adapting some facilities and or making other alternative arrangements and reasonable accommodations in accordance with the Americans with Disabilities Act (1990, S. 933).

Child Care Center Building

Because the structure and design of the child care center building have a marked influence on the type of program that can be offered to the children and their families, the building should be designed to promote safe and appropriate program activities for the children. The size and location of the rooms should contribute to the comfort and activities of children and adults alike.

New buildings should be planned so that the facilities will be functional and flexible. The interior and exterior finish materials and colors should enhance the comfort of children and staff. Visual clutter should be kept to a minimum by using closed cabinets, closets, and storage areas both inside and outside. Cabinets should be selected and organized so children are encouraged to choose developmentally appropriate materials. Spaces should be designed to reduce noise and distraction between groups.

Many school-age and some preschool programs are located in public and private elementary school buildings. All standards that deal with child care center-based programs also apply to school-based programs. School-based programs should have age-appropriate equipment and materials, and should undergo the same regular inspections as center-based programs.

3.4   Location of the Child Care Center Facilities

The child care service should ensure that child care center facilities, with outdoor space for children to play safely both in active and passive activities (e.g., gardening, storytelling, playing in a sandbox), are accessible to the families that can benefit from them.

Neighborhood-based or school-based programs serving local communities or employer-based programs serving a work community and accessible to public transportation are most appropriate. The location should be chosen to limit the children's exposure to violence, drug paraphernalia or dealing, and prostitution.

When transportation is provided by the child care service, children younger than 6 years of age should not travel more than 45 minutes daily each way.

3.5   External Environment

The child care service facility should be in an environment that is safe, and its external appearance should be attractive, well maintained, and comparable to other residences in the area. The grounds of the facility should be free of any contamination of the soil or air and protected from excessive traffic noise.

3.6   Structure and Safety of the Building

The child care service should ensure that the building used for a child care center is sound in structure, safe for use by groups of children, and in compliance with state and local building and fire codes.

The following factors should be taken into consideration as well:

Special risks are involved in caring for very young children or those with special needs in groups; these needs may not be recognized in municipal regulations for other buildings, but should be considered by the child care service.

For the group care of young children, ground floor quarters are most appropriate. In buildings with automatic sprinkler systems and at least two unobstructed exits to the outside designated solely for the use of the children in the child care center, a second floor location may be allowed.

Space above the second floor of a facility should be used only if an elevator is provided, if provision is made for prompt evacuation of the children in case of an emergency, and if the space is in accordance with licensing and fire code regulations. Fire escapes are essential if children are cared for above the first floor.

In some regions, building codes do not permit the use of spaces above the ground floor for the care of children in child care, preschool, kindergarten, or first and second grades. Rooms below street level should not be used unless at-grade exits are provided and the spaces have adequate natural light, exterior views, and ventilation.

If an elevator transports children to and from classrooms, monthly professional inspection and maintenance should be added to the regular, municipal inspections.

On each floor, at least two widely separated, unobstructed exits should lead directly outdoors as an essential safety measure. The number of exits, and locations and distances between these exists, should be determined by local building codes.

All stairways, including fire escapes, should have protected sides and be constructed with low risers and broad treads. Handrail size, spacing, and height on stairs and ramps should be according to code. In addition, a handrail must be placed at a lower than standard height for use by children.

All windows in the rooms used by children should have guards of the proper height and type to protect children from falling out. Windows should extend close enough to the floor to provide natural ventilation and admit outdoor sounds.

Electrical outlets should be above child height or protected by special safety caps. In older buildings, electrical wiring should be inspected regularly for signs of deterioration, and repaired and/or replaced as necessary.

The furnace or central burner should be completely enclosed in a secured room of fireproof construction and should be inspected regularly.

In new buildings, all materials should be fire resistant. Older buildings should be made as fire resistant as possible and as required by codes, with attention to requirements for smoke detectors, rate-of-temperature-rise alarms, and automatic sprinkler systems.

Older buildings should be inspected for asbestos. If it is found, it should be encapsulated or removed.

Paints used for both indoor and outdoor play structures should be checked for lead content to be certain they are in compliance with state and federal laws. Paint and other finishes should be easily washable. Vinyl wall coverings can provide more durable and low maintenance finishes for walls than paint.

Fire extinguishers should be placed above child height for preschoolers but should be accessible to adults. They should be in all rooms used by children, as well as in the kitchen and reception area. All extinguishers should be tested regularly.

A fire alarm system is desirable and may be required in any building used by groups of young children.

Where regular inspection of the premises by the building and fire departments is not required by law, the child care service should request an annual inspection to promote an awareness of the need for caution and necessary improvements.

3.7   Sanitation

The child care service should ensure that the center's buildings comply with all state and local sanitation requirements, and with any other special measures required as safeguards when young children are cared for in groups.

Additional measures include:

- The water supply, including hot and cold water, and the method of sewage disposal should be approved by the local sanitation authority.

- Dishwashing procedures and facilities should follow U.S. Food and Nutrition Service sanitation standards. Dishes should be sterilized with water at a temperature of at least 180°F. Chemical sterilization is acceptable. Either method depends on thorough rinsing to avoid soap or chemical residue on dishes.

- When a temperature of 180°F for dishwashing is not possible, paper or other disposable materials should be supplied for serving food.

- Adequate handwashing facilities, in sufficient number and of a sanitary type, should be provided separately for children and adults.

- Sanitary drinking water should be available to all children, both inside and outside. Rather than a drinking fountain, faucets and paper cups should be used for preschool children.
- Windows and doors should be screened and securely fastened against insects.
- Floors and walls should be covered with materials that can be frequently washed and easily maintained, and should be kept clean.
- Food storage facilities should include a refrigerator and dry ventilated storage space for fresh and dry foods not requiring refrigeration. A temperature of 40°F or lower should be maintained in all food storage areas, with the exception of freezers, which should be maintained at 0°F. A thermometer should be placed in all food storage areas.
  - Appropriate storage of food and a clean environment will help control pests. An exterminator should be used to control any insects and pests. Exposure to pesticides and pesticide residue by small children who spend time playing on the floor should be avoided.

3.8   Disposition of Space

The child care service should ensure that space in the child care center building is sufficient to meet the needs and purposes of the center.

In planning the disposition of space, consideration should be given to the need for:

- a playroom for each group of children, reserved exclusively for their use during the hours they are in the building;
- separate areas from food service areas for diaper changing;
- kitchen facilities;
- storage for food, equipment, and office supplies;
- a reception area;

- a staff lounge;
- a get-well room for mildly ill children;
- a laundry room (if serving infants and toddlers);
- toilet rooms for adults and children, adjacent to the playrooms;
- a janitor's room with a mop sink and locked storage for cleaning supplies;
- closet space for adult's coats;
- room for large muscle motor activities if climate limits the amount of time that can be spent outdoors;
- containers to sort trash for recycling and space to store them (optional); and
- separate rooms and facilities for preschool and school-age children with separated entrances or different buildings if possible.

3.9   Toilet and Handwashing Facilities and Diaper Changing Areas

The child care service facility should have one toilet and one handwashing sink for every ten children, with separate toilet and handwashing facilities for adults. Toilet facilities should be accessible to physically challenged children.

Toilets and handwashing sinks scaled for children should be permanently installed and secured, and should be of appropriate height for the comfort of the children and for helping them to develop skills in caring for themselves.

Nonflushing potty-chairs used in toilet training should be discouraged. The child care center should provide modifications to adult-size toilets or permanent child-size toilets in its toddler areas to assist in toilet training.

Toilet and handwashing facilities should be directly accessible to the playroom and to the outdoor play area. An unlocked door should separate the playroom from the toilet facility to prevent unaccompanied toddlers from entering the toilet facility. This is particularly important when programs serve both toddlers and preschoolers.

The wall and floor finishes in toilet rooms should be made of ceramic tile or other easily cleanable, nonpermeable material. The room should be of adequate size to allow several children and adult staff members access at the same time.

Children younger than 5 should have an adult accompany them to the toilet facility. For children 6 and older, separate facilities for boys and girls should be available.

Water used by children for washing should have an automatic control to prevent the temperature from rising above 120°F. If permitted by code, the child care service should consider reducing the maximum temperature to 105°F for younger children. Faucets should be operated by knee/foot pedal or electric eye to maintain sanitary conditions.

Disposable hand towels should be used for drying hands

Diaper changing surfaces should be covered with a disposable impermeable cover that is changed after each use and disposed of in a closed container. The changing surface should be washed, disinfected, and allowed to air dry after each use and should not be used for any other purpose. Running water should be adjacent to the diapering area for hand washing. The standards for infection control found in *Caring for Our Children: National Health and Safety Performance Standards* (U.S. DHHS, Maternal and Child Health Bureau, 2002) should be followed.

Soiled disposable diapers should be placed in a closed container lined with a leakproof disposable lining. Soiled nondisposable diapers should be placed in a sealed plastic container labeled with the child's name and returned to the parents. Some regulations and codes may not allow nondisposable soiled diapers to be returned to parents. In such instances, an independent company should handle nondisposable soiled diapers. All soiled diapers should be removed from the center daily.

Other nondisposable materials that may be used (e.g., towels, washcloths) should be kept in a sanitary condition and hung at the child's height, with sufficient space between them to prevent them from touching.

3.10 Kitchen Facilities

The child care service should ensure that kitchen facilities in the child care center building are sanitary, orderly, well lit, well ventilated, conveniently located, and properly equipped for serving food to groups of children.

The kitchen should be completely closed off and separated from the playrooms, yet located so that food can be transported readily and served while hot.

Walls and floors of rooms where food is prepared and stored should be easy to clean. A sink for handwashing should be accessible to the kitchen staff and liquid soap should be available.

The kitchen should have an adjacent storeroom that is properly equipped with staples and canned foods.

The kitchen should have separate areas for food preparation, cooking, serving, and cleanup.

The kitchen should have the appropriate equipment for refrigeration of perishable foods, sterilization of dishes, and cooking utensils, and a sanitary method of disposing of garbage.

The child care service should comply with local health regulations for food handlers and for the care and service of food for children in groups outside their own homes.

A well-equipped kitchen is essential to good food service. The kitchen should include:

- appropriate food storage that is separate from storage for cleaning supplies and equipment;
- hot water temperatures and equipment for cleaning and sterilizing dishes and utensils;
- adequate lighting and mechanisms for controlling heat and odors;
- walls, floors, and food preparation surfaces that are attractive and easy to clean;
- first aid supplies; and
- a fire extinguisher.

3.11 Space for Staff Offices and Parent Meetings

The child care center building should have sufficient space for staff offices and for meetings of administrators, staff members, and parents.

The child care center building's offices provide a first impression of the child care center to families and other visitors. Offices should be attractive and have all the necessary equipment for communication, business, and special purposes.

The child care center building should have a reception room with comfortable furniture, toys for children, and reading materials for parents and other adults visiting the center. Materials should be available in the languages most frequently spoken by the children and families served.

The child care center building should have a comfortable and attractively furnished room for staff members' rest period, and meetings of staff members, parents, or board members. In a large center, however, a separate room for various meetings may be preferred.

The child care center building should have office space for private interviews with parents and for staff conferences. Offices should have the equipment necessary to facilitate the administration of the child care service. Space should be allocated for files and the storage of office supplies.

When physical examinations are given in the child care center, a special room for this purpose should be set aside and properly equipped, lit, heated, and ventilated. Additional office space may be required for conferences between the doctor or nurse and parents.

3.12 Isolation Space for the Ill Child

The child care center building should have a separate space for the isolation of children when an acute illness occurs.

The space for isolation should be located close to a staff member so that the child may be observed and will not feel alone. It may be adjacent to the office assigned to the health personnel or in the room used for first aid or physical examinations. In a small center, it may be a corner in the office of the director, social worker, or secretary.

If first aid supplies are stored in the space used for isolation, they should be kept in a secure container out of the reach of children.

Bathroom facilities should be easily accessible to the space used for sick children.

The Children's Play Space (Playroom)

The children's play space in the child care center building should be planned so that the activities of daily living for each child can be carried out with friends and in familiar surroundings. Suitable and interesting equipment should be available at all times for appropriate activities throughout the day, such as work, play, rest, meals, and snacks.

The child care center facility should have a warm, friendly atmosphere and should be physically comfortable and aesthetically pleasing. Walls in soft, light colors, decorated with children's work at their eye level, and an uncluttered and orderly arrangement of equipment and furnishings will have a beneficial and lasting influence on the children.

The equipment and its arrangement should contribute to the quality of the program and to the attainment of the objectives of the child care service.

Different types of play call for both vinyl and carpeted floor areas, and for a variety of lighting levels, both natural and artificial. When possible, the play space should be open so children can be visible at all times.

3.13 Size of the Playroom

The child care center building should have a ratio of 50 square feet of playroom floor space per child including cribs, lofts, and quality play equipment, but exclusive of the space occupied by sinks, lockers, and storage cabinets, for the activities and comfort of the children.

Each playroom for a group of 15 children should have 750 square feet of floor space, in addition to the area occupied by such fixed equipment as sinks or lockers. The size of the playroom should limit the number of children who can use it, in accordance with the standards governing the size of groups.

Playrooms in a child care center buildings should offer sufficient room for a variety of activities to take place simultaneously, without the children crowding each other.

Space should be available for the conduct of large-muscle motor activities, especially where climate limits the amount of time that can be spent outdoors. The ages and needs of the children served by the child care center should determine the maximum amount of space needed. For example, children with physical handicaps may require more than the minimum space requirements for the use of therapeutic equipment, while the infants' and toddlers' space may not require more than the minimum square footage because they are not yet fully mobile.

3.14 Temperature of the Playroom

The child care service should ensure that the playroom in the child care center maintains a temperature of 68°F to 80°F, as measured two feet off the floor. Each playroom should have a nonmercury thermometer.

Air conditioning is desirable in hot weather or hot climates.

The child care center should have central heating, with recessed radiators, if at all possible.

All exposed radiators should have a protective covering.

Portable heaters and open fires are prohibited. Stoves should be fastened permanently to the floor or wall and screened so children cannot touch them.

3.15 Light and Ventilation in the Playroom

The child care service should ensure that each playroom in the child care center has outside windows, the total area of which is at least 10% of the floor area.

Windows low enough for children to look out of should be used because they are a source of pleasure and learning. Higher windows should be equipped with platforms on which children can stand. All windows should have proper protection against falling.

Adjustable shades should be used in each room to provide protection from glare, and to produce an atmosphere conducive to relaxation at rest time.

The playroom of the child care center should be adequately ventilated and draft free. Air conditioning should be used if windows do not provide sufficient natural ventilation or in warm climates. Fans may be used if they are properly protected and secured.

The child care center should use artificial lighting of at least 35 footcandle power. For reading and close work, lighting of 50 to 100 foot candles is recommended. Lights should be equipped with dimming switches so light levels can be easily varied within the space. Consideration should be given to a combination of fluorescent and incandescent light sources.

3.16 Soundproofing

The child care service should ensure that materials that help to control sound are used for the playroom ceiling and walls.

Sound-absorbing ceilings should be used.

Soundproofing material in the exterior walls should be used if the center is located in a multipurpose structure or close to other buildings. Sound insulation systems applied within walls and above ceilings are less expensive and more effective than those applied to the finished faces of the room.

3.17 Playroom Flooring

The child care service should ensure that floors in all rooms used by children are covered with a smooth, splinter-proof material, such as linoleum, vinyl tile, or fire-code-approved carpeting.

Floor coverings should differ to accommodate separate areas for messy, active play and for quieter activities.

3.18 Playroom Equipment, Furnishings, and Materials

The child care service should select equipment, furnishings, and materials in the playroom on the basis of their suitability for the children who will use them, their durability, and their adaptability to various uses.

The ages, developmental levels, and interests of the children should be considered in furnishing and equipping the children's playroom.

Equipment and materials should be regarded as tools for the developmental tasks and educational experiences that help children value themselves (see 1.6–1.9). They should be plentiful, attractive, clean, and in good repair. Furnishings such as tables, chairs, low open shelving, individual lockers for children's belongings, light stackable cots, play materials, and equipment for food service should be appropriate in height, size, and design for the comfort, health, safety, and developmental needs of the children in the group.

Materials that children can manage, move, and change should be used because they contribute more to growth and development than those of limited use or flexibility.

- Nonbreakable mirrors provide opportunities to enhance self-image through dramatic play.
- A sink or other readily available source of water should be handy for such activities as housekeeping play, creative arts, and science.
- Plants and pets in the play space give children an opportunity to observe and become involved in life processes (see *Caring for Our Children: National Health and Safety Performance Standards*, Chapter 5, U.S. DHHS, Maternal and Child Health Bureau, 2002).

3.19   Arrangement of the Playroom

The child care service should ensure that furnishings, equipment, and materials of the child care center building are arranged into orderly, clearly defined areas of interest, with sufficient space in each for the children to see the various activities available to them.

The playroom should have learning areas for dramatic play, block building, creative arts, books, table games, puzzles, music, science, and multimedia activities (e.g., computers, woodworking).

Shelving should facilitate order and place the materials within easy reach of the children. The equipment should be arranged in a manner that suggests how it should be used, and should offer easy opportunities for a child to meet with success in whatever activity is selected.

Orderly, clearly defined areas established within the play space help children develop a sense of order and encourage them to take responsibility for maintaining it.

Equipment should be in good supply and easily available. Its arrangement should suggest activities and invite a child to explore. It should help each child make choices, see relationships, organize ideas, and solve problems.

The following principles should guide the arrangement of the room's equipment:

- Furnishings and equipment used together should be grouped together in the same room.
- Activities requiring close eye work should be located in the best-lit areas of the room.
- Activities requiring protection from foot traffic (e.g., block building) should be out of high-traffic areas.
- Quiet activities should be located together, away from active play areas.
- All areas should be arranged so that the teacher/care provider can supervise appropriately at all times.
- Adjustments in the layout of the room and the type of equipment used should be made for children with special needs.

The Children's Outdoor Play Area

Outdoor play is not only important for children's health, but is also an integral part of their learning experiences. Outdoor play space should offer opportunities for adventure, challenge, and wonder in the natural environment. The child care center that cares for children for a major part of the day should have a playground of its own. It should be planned with flexibility and imagination so that growth and learning can take place within it and should be suitable for the various needs of the children served, the particular climate, and its urban or rural location. If it is necessary for

the child care service to use a public playground for outdoor play, the playground should be in compliance with
the same standards as if it were the center's own play area.

3.20 Location of the Outdoor Play Area

The child care service should ensure that the playground ad-
joins the child care center building and is directly accessible to
each playroom, so that indoor and outdoor play can be inter-
changeable. The playground area should be easily observed from
the building's classrooms or offices for additional security.

School-age children may use community facilities for outdoor play under supervision of child care staff members.

3.21 Size of the Outdoor Play Area

The child care service should ensure that the child care center provides a minimum of 75 square feet of outdoor space
per child, with a variety of equipment, both large and small,
stationary and moveable, to permit active play for each group
of children.

An area of at least 1,125 square feet, or a lot equivalent to
about 35 feet by 32 feet, is recommended for a group of 15
children. In crowded, urban environments, it may be necessary to use a smaller space, but it should not provide less
then 50 square feet per child. In situations where space or
climate limit outdoor play time, a large, multipurpose indoor room should be considered to allow for rigorous physical activity. If necessary because of space limitations, the
use of the playground by different age groups of children
should be scheduled to ensure that all children have access
to the outdoor area designated for their active play.

If two or more age groups of children must use the same
playground at the same time, it should be large enough to
separate the groups so that the children of each group can
have access to appropriate equipment and space.

3.22 Physical Requirements for the Playground

The child care service should ensure that the playground of the
child care center is safe and comfortable, with a resilient surface suitable for the activities that will take place on it.

The playground should be well drained, and have surfaces appropriate for wheeled toys, soft ground for digging/planting, and resilient surfacing for zones in which falls may occur.

The playground should have an area shaded by either trees or awnings, and a covered area for inclement weather.

The playground should be accessible to a safe source of water and to toilet facilities.

The playground for preschool children should be protected by non-scalable fencing at least four feet in height. If the playground is on a roof, the fence should be six feet high.

In windy areas, or where privacy is desired, a semisolid fence should be used for protection.

3.23 Playground Equipment

The child care service should select outdoor play equipment for the child care center on the same basis as used for indoor equipment, in accordance with the ages, interests, and skills of the children who use it.

Special consideration should be given to opportunities outdoor play equipment can provide for vigorous activity and contact with the physical world.

The installation of large stationary equipment should conform to local safety regulations. Concrete foundations should extend at least 18 inches into the ground.

The surface under all climbing or other stationary equipment (e.g., slides, swings, seesaws, etc.) should be soft and resilient. Swing seats should be of canvas, leather, or rubber.

Equipment should be in good repair and inspected continuously using a maintenance checklist.

Children should be provided with adequate supervision and protection appropriate to the activity they are engaged in or the equipment they are using. For example, children may be required to wear an approved or certified helmet when riding bikes or have added adult supervision when using monkey bars. Children should be visible to those supervising them at all times.

Sandboxes, if used, should be covered with a lid when not in use and maintained in sanitary conditions by regularly replacing the sand. The child care service should follow *Caring for Our Children: National Health and Safety Performance Standards*, Standard 5.180 (U.S. DHHS, Maternal and Child Health Bureau, 2002) on the use of sandboxes.

Sprinklers are recommended for outdoor water play. If a wading pool is used for outdoor water play, it should be maintained in sanitary conditions, or other facilities for water play should be considered in the outdoor program during warm weather. If pools are onsite, they should not be accessible to children when not in use. A fence should surround pools and be at least six feet high. Entrances to the pool should remain locked at all times and the pool should have a secure cover over it when not in use. When a pool is in use, staff should be appropriately trained in water safety and should maintain low teacher-child ratios. The child care service should comply with all the standards on swimming, wading, and water *of Caring for Our Children: National Health and Safety Performance Standards*, Standard 5.4 (U.S. DHHS, Maternal and Child Health Bureau, 2002).

3.24 Arrangement of Outdoor Area

The child care service should arrange the outdoor equipment and accessory materials, together with facilities for storage, in orderly, clearly defined areas of interest, suitable for the use of particular equipment.

In planning the various play areas, the child care service should consider the kinds of surfaces needed, the amount of space required to provide a satisfying experience for children using the equipment, and the distance between pieces of equipment necessary to allow for a safe and rewarding pursuit of the activity.

At least one-quarter of the playground space should be free of playground equipment to allow for running, climbing, swinging, digging, gardening, building, riding wheeled toys, playing ball, and in warm weather, playing in a wading pool.

In a roof playground, climbing equipment should be kept away from the fence.

Swings should be placed so that children engaged in other activities have no occasion to run near them. They should have a clearance of six feet surrounding them.

Storage facilities on the playground should be designed not only to protect but also to make the equipment for the activity easily accessible.

Family Child Care Homes and Group Child Care Homes

Family and group child care homes should strive to achieve the same standards of excellence set forward for child care centers, with a few changes to accommodate for the differences in their services.

3.25 Family Child Care Home and Group Child Care Home Buildings

The child care service should ensure that the physical facilities of the family child care home or group child care home supply adequate space for the daily activities of young children, and present no hazards to their health or safety.

3.26 Location of the Family or Group Child Care Home

The child care service should ensure that the family child care home or group child care home is located in a safe environment that is friendly and welcoming to children and families.

The location should be chosen to limit children's exposure to violence and criminal activity. When the family child care provider is located in a higher risk environment, the child care service should assist the provider and parents in taking needed precautions to assure the safety of all involved.

Attention also should be given to the environmental issues described in section 3.5.

3.27 Structure and Safety of the Family or Group Child Care Home

The child care service should ensure that family or group child care homes are sound in structure, safe for use by groups, and in compliance with state and local building codes.

Dwellings should conform to state and local health, fire, and sanitary regulations.

Homes should undergo regular fire inspections, even if not required by the state or locality, and maintain smoke and carbon monoxide detectors along with fire extinguishers in all rooms, out of the reach of children.

Home should be inspected for asbestos. If it is found, it should be encapsulated or removed.

Paints used both indoors and outdoors should be lead free in compliance with federal and state laws.

If the child care home is housed in an apartment building, proper safety provisions should be taken. Low railings and protected sides should be installed in stairways, as well as bars on hallway windows.

Electrical outlets should be above child height or protected by special safety caps. In older buildings, electrical wiring should be inspected regularly for signs of deterioration, and repaired and/or replaced as necessary.

3.28 Sanitation

The child care service should ensure that the family and group child care home complies with all requirements of the state and local sanitation authorities, and with any other special measures required as safeguards when young children are cared for in groups.

Water should be sanitary and of satisfactory quality for drinking and household use, with a safe and adequate supply for washing and bathing. Water from springs, wells, or other private sources should be protected against contamination. The health department should always test water that is not from a tested public supply.

Dishwashing procedures and facilities should follow U.S. Food and Nutrition Service sanitation standards. Dishes should be sterilized with water at a temperature of at least 180°F. Chemical sterilization is acceptable. Either method depends on thorough rinsing to avoid soap or chemical residue on dishes.

When a temperature of 180°F for dishwashing is not possible, paper or other disposable materials should be supplied for serving food.

Food storage facilities should include a refrigerator and dry ventilated storage space for fresh and dry foods not requiring refrigeration. A temperature of 40°F or lower should be maintained in all food storage areas, with the exception of freezers, which should be maintained at 0°F. A thermometer should be placed in all food storage areas.

- Appropriate storage of food and a clean environment will help control pests. An exterminator should be used to control any insects and pests. Exposure to pesticides and pesticide residue by small children who spend time playing on the floor should be avoided.

Floors and walls should be covered with materials that can be frequently washed and easily maintained, and should be kept clean.

Windows and doors should be screened and securely fastened against insects.

Proper provisions should be made for food preparation, care of perishable food, and refrigeration, especially of milk, meats, and poultry.

3.29 Disposition of Space

The child care service should ensure that space in the family or group child care home is sufficient to meet the needs and purposes of the home.

The family child care home or group home should have a playroom for the children, in addition to separate areas for food preparation and diaper changing.

The family child care home or group home should have an isolation room or area for sick children and adequate toilet and handwashing facilities.

The family or group child care home may not have as much variety in rooms as a child care center, but should work to make sure all the needs of the children served are met.

3.30 Toilet and Handwashing Facilities and Diaper Changing Areas

The child care service should ensure that family and group child care homes include one toilet and one handwashing sink for every 10 children, with separate toilet and handwashing facilities for adults if possible.

Nonflushing potty chairs used in toilet training should be discouraged. The home should provide modifications to adult-sized toilets or permanent child-size toilets to assist in toilet training.

Toilet and handwashing facilities should be accessible to the playroom. A door should separate the playroom from the toilet facility. An adult should accompany toddlers and preschoolers under the age of five into the toilet facility.

Water used by children to wash their hands should be set at a temperature of 120°F or below to prevent accidental scalding. Disposable hand towels should be used for drying hands.

Diaper changing surfaces should be covered with a disposable impermeable cover that is changed after each use and disposed of in a closed container. The changing surface should be washed, disinfected, and allowed to air dry after each use and not used for any other purpose.

Soiled disposable diapers should be placed in a closed container lined with a leakproof disposable lining. Soiled nondisposable diapers should be placed in a sealed plastic container labeled with the child's name and returned to the parents. Some regulations and codes may not allow nondisposable soiled diapers to be returned to parents. In such instances, an independent company should handle nondisposable soiled diapers. All soiled diapers should be removed from the home daily.

Other nondisposable materials that may be used (e.g., towels, washcloths) should be kept in a sanitary condition and hung at the child's height, with sufficient space between them to prevent them from touching.

3.31 Kitchen Facilities

The child care service should ensure that kitchen facilities in the family or group child care home are sanitary, orderly, well lit, well ventilated, conveniently located, and properly equipped.

The kitchen should be closed off and separated from the playrooms, yet located so that food can be transported and served while still hot.

A sink for handwashing and liquid soap should be easily accessible.

The kitchen should have an adjacent storeroom that is properly equipped with staples and canned foods.

The kitchen should have the appropriate equipment for refrigeration of perishable foods, sterilization of dishes, and cooking utensils, and a sanitary method of disposing of garbage.

A well-equipped kitchen is essential to good food service. The kitchen should include:

- appropriate food storage that is separate from storage for cleaning supplies and equipment;
- hot water temperatures and equipment for cleaning and sterilizing dishes and utensils;
- microwave ovens (if used) that are inaccessible to preschool-age children;
- adequate lighting and mechanisms for controlling heat and odors;
- walls, floors, and food preparation surfaces that are attractive and easy to clean;
- first aid supplies; and
- a fire extinguisher.

3.32 Isolation Space for the Ill Child

The child care service should ensure that family and group child care homes have a separate space for the isolation of children when an acute illness occurs.

The space for isolation should be located close to where the provider will be so that child may be observed and will not feel alone.

Bathroom facilities should be easily accessible to the space used for sick children.

3.33 The Playroom in Family or Group Child Care Homes

The child care service should plan the children's play space so that the activities of daily living for each child can be with friends and in familiar surroundings.

Suitable and interesting equipment should be available at all times for appropriate activities throughout the day, such as work, play, rest, meals, and snacks.

3.34 Size of the Playroom

The child care service should ensure that a minimum of 35 square feet of usable space is available per child in the family child care home or group home.

3.35 Temperature of Playroom

The child care service should ensure that heating and cooling, ventilating, and lighting facilities are adequate to protect the health of children.

A temperature of 68°F to 80°F (measured two feet from the floor) should be maintained in all rooms occupied by children.

In hot weather and in hot climates, air conditioning should be used.

Fans, properly protected, may be used.

Radiators and other heat sources should be protected to prevent burns. As with center-based programs, open fires, use of ovens for heat, and portable heaters should be prohibited.

3.36 Light and Ventilation in the Playroom

The child care service should ensure that all rooms used for children have sufficient sunlight, with windows above street level.

Windows above the first five feet of the building should be fitted with guards. Windows and doors should be effectively screened against flies, mosquitoes, and other insects.

3.37 Soundproofing

The child care service should ensure that materials that help control sound are used in the playroom ceilings and walls of family child care homes or group homes.

3.38 Playroom Flooring

The child care service should ensure that floors in all rooms used by children are covered with a smooth, splinter-proof material, such as linoleum, vinyl tile, or fire-code approved carpeting.

> Floor coverings should differ to accommodate separate areas for messy and active play and for quieter activities. Area rugs should be secured.

3.39 Playroom Equipment, Furnishings, and Materials

As in the child care center, the child care service should ensure that equipment, furnishings, and materials in the family or group child care home are selected on the basis of their suitability for the children who will use them, their durability, and their adaptability to various uses.

> Table and chairs should be comfortable for the children who use them. Any heavy furniture should be securely anchored or stable.

> Enough toys should be available to engage all children in developmentally appropriate play.

> Materials should be stored in consistent places that are easy for children to reach.

> Materials and toys should promote understanding and acceptance of differences, including culture, ethnicity, and gender.

3.40 Arrangement of the Playroom

The child care service should ensure that furnishings, equipment, and materials of the family or group child care home are arranged into orderly, clearly defined areas of interest, with sufficient space in each for the children to see the various activities available to them.

Orderly, clearly defined areas established within the play space help children develop a sense of order and encourage them to take responsibility for managing it.

Household cleaning supplies, knives, chemicals, and medicines should be kept locked up and safely out of the reach of the children.

3.41 Firearms

The child care service should ensure that any firearms in a family or group child care home are locked, unloaded, and inaccessible to children. Ammunition should be stored in a locked case, separate from the firearm and also inaccessible to children. Parents should be notified if there is a firearm at the home.

3.42 Sleeping Arrangements in the Family Child Care Home and Group Child Care Home

The child care service should ensure that the family child care home or group child care home provides each child younger than 6 years of age with individual sleeping accommodations that are kept clean and sanitary at all times, and with adequate bedding suitable to the season and climate.

If there is more than one child in the home, sufficient room must be available to permit the temporary isolation of a child in the event of illness.

3.43 Pets/Animals in the Family or Group Child Care Home

The child care service should ensure that pets in the family or group child care homes do not include ferrets, turtles, iguanas, lizards or other reptiles, birds of the parrot family (*psittacine*), or any wild animals.

If pets are in the home, the facility should have a written policy about their care and adhere to this and any state or local regulations for care of pets.

All pet supplies shall be kept out of reach of children, especially food and litter.

Cages should be approved and regularly checked.

Children and care providers should wash their hands after handling the animals and animals should be prohibited from all food preparation or serving areas.

The family child care provider should comply with *Caring for Our Children: National Health and Safety Performance Standards*, Standards 3.042-3.044 (U.S. DHHS, Maternal and Child Health Bureau, 2002) on pets and animals in a child care setting.

3.44 Location and Size of the Outdoor Play Area

The child care service should ensure that children have access to adequate outdoor space that is within walking distance of the family or group child care home.

Children should be carefully supervised when walking to and from the play space in addition to the supervision provided at the playground or outdoor space.

3.45 Physical Requirements for the Outdoor Play Area

The child care service should apply the same rules and suggestions that apply to the outdoor space of a center to those for family child care homes and group homes (see 3.22).

3.46 Playground Equipment

The child care service should apply the same rules and suggestions that apply to the outdoor space of a center to those for family child care homes and group homes (see 3.23).

3.47 Arrangement of Playground

The child care service should apply the same rules and suggestions that apply to the outdoor space of a center to those for family child care homes and group child care homes (see 3.24).

4

Staffing the Child Care Service

Goals

    I. The child care service hires, retains, and develops competent, qualified, diverse staff to administer, manage, and deliver child care services.

    II. All staff of the child care service have clearly defined roles and provide care in accordance with the philosophy, goals, and policies of the child care service.

    III. Orientation and inservice training provided to staff ensure that staff have the knowledge and understanding of the needs of children and their families and the skills to provide appropriate, culturally competent care and education.

    IV. Salaries and benefits in child care services are sufficient to attract and retain highly qualified staff and are comparable to those for other positions of equal responsibility.

    V. Group size and staff-child care ratios are consistent with those recommended by the body of research to produce high quality child care.

To accomplish its purpose and goals, the child care service requires the collaboration of all its staff members working as a team. Each member of the child care service staff should have a clearly defined role in ensuring that the essential components are provided in a manner in which individual children and their parents receive an effectively integrated service.

The child care service may be a stand-alone service or a part of a multiservice agency.

The child care service may employ a variety of staff ranging from Aides to Directors to Consultants. Child care services will differ in their use of titles for each position. For consistency, the following progression of roles for both stand-alone and multiservice agencies are used:

- Agency Director
- Manager
- Center Director
- Teacher
- Assistant Teacher
- Aide
- Volunteer/Student Intern

Staffing Responsibilities and Skills Required

4.1   Shared Responsibilities of All Staff Members

All staff members of the child care service should have clearly defined roles and should conduct their responsibilities in accordance with the plan for each child and family and within the framework of the goals, purposes, and policies of the child care service.

Staff members should work toward the goals and purposes of the service and should be aware of how their work contributes to the service's overall mission.

Staff members should recognize and actively advocate for the primary significance of the child-parent relationship, the importance of the parents' participation as partners in the program, and the role of the child care service in supporting and strengthening the child-parent relationship.

Staff members should cooperate in the development and implementation of the care plan for the children and families with whom they work, as well as in evaluating the benefits obtained by the children and families from the service, and in determining whether the need for child care is being met appropriately.

Staff members should contribute pertinent information from daily observations to each child's care records.

Staff members should have the opportunity to observe the child, parents, and other family members and to learn what is happening at home and in the child care program.

Staff members, within their given roles in the child care service, should provide support to parents with respect to problems that may occur in the course of the parents' rearing of their children.

4.2   Responsibilities and Skills Needed for Various Positions in the Child Care Service

The child care service should obtain the knowledge and skills of a range of professional workers to implement an effective child care service.

Due to gaps in the availability of training for child care providers, many child care providers do not have direct access to opportunities for professional preparation. The child care service, as an employer of child care providers, should help its staff members obtain appropriate professional training.

The child care service should determine the requirements for a given position on the basis of the responsibilities and skills involved. Staff positions vary among different forms of child care. The same position title within a given agency may carry different responsibilities and therefore require different levels of professional certification and experience.

Professional certification is available at several levels, including the child development associate credential (a one-year certificate), associate's degree (a two-year program), bachelor's degree, and graduate degree.

In addition, preservice preparation offering the basic skills required for the position to be held should be provided before the worker begins work with the children.

Regular inservice training should be provided to develop the particular skills required by the child care service for its own program.

Continuing education, especially in regard to new developments in the field, should be provided and required for all child care professionals regardless of the level of their formal education.

All forms of child care training programs should provide and require formal, generally acceptable credentials for all their trainees. The training programs should include opportunities for staff members to improve their level of cultural competency, as well as provide information necessary to serve children with special needs who may be using the service.

4.3   Responsibilities Required of the Director of the Agency with a Child Care Service Component

The child care service should ensure that the responsibilities of the director of the agency include leadership, planning, and administration; recordkeeping; regulatory compliance; service coordination; fund development; and service as a liaison to various constituencies.

The director of the agency with a child care service component is responsible for:

- providing leadership;
- planning and administering a culturally competent cost-effective service;
- administering a fiscally responsible agency;
- maintaining complete and accurate financial and administrative records;
- ensuring compliance with regulatory professional and facility requirements;
- ensuring functionality and quality of all aspects of the agency, including the child care service;
- ensuring that all components are coordinated to accomplish the goals of the service;
- finding and using community resources for fundraising and grants as well as services to children and families;
- ensuring that the program is appropriately staffed to deliver services;

- representing the agency in the community;
- responding to the changing needs of the community by adapting programs;
- serving as a liaison between staff members and board members and between staff members and the community; and
- keeping both staff members and board members informed of pertinent legislative and regulatory matters.

4.4 Skills Required by the Director of the Agency with a Child Care Service Component

The child care service should ensure that the director of the agency possesses leadership qualities, including a sense of vision and a philosophic perspective that reflects the board of directors' policy directions, is culturally competent and sensitive, and is able to set the tone for the agency. The director should have at least an undergraduate degree in early childhood development or a related field as well as experience in the field and additional training. A graduate-level degree in the field is encouraged.

In large agencies, where the director's responsibilities are strictly administrative, the qualifications should also emphasize business administration. Bearing in mind that these individuals are in charge of agencies that include components other than child care, they should have experience and degrees in fields related to the overall work of their agency but do not necessarily need specific training or experience in child care.

4.5 Responsibilities of Managers of the Components of the Child Care Service

The child care service should ensure that the responsibilities of managers of the components of the child care service include planning and administering the assigned component of the service, ensuring that appropriate staff members and supervisors or consultants are available, and serving as a liaison between supervisors and the director of the agency.

4.6   Skills Required by Managers of the Components of the Child Care Service

The child care service should ensure that the managers of components of the child care service meet all of the requirements of lead teachers and supervisors, as described below, and, in addition, have at least six months of subsequent work experience. Managers should possess both education and experience in administration, and, where the component is specialized, credentials reflecting the needs of the specialized component (e.g., recreational sciences for school-age child care; mental health resources for therapeutic child care settings).

4.7   Responsibilities of the Center Directors for the Child Care Service

The child care service should ensure that the responsibilities of the center director in the child care service include: monitoring scheduling, staffing, and program activities; working with staff members to enhance the service; identifying problems and helping staff members to develop a plan to deal with them; making scheduled observations and evaluations of individual staff performance; promoting parent involvement; coordinating health and development services for children with their primary health care provider; and coordinating with other services such as schools, special education services, and mental health care providers.

4.8   Skills Required by Center Directors of the Child Care Service

The child care service should ensure that center directors in the child care service have interpersonal skills that enable them to give effective guidance to teachers/care providers, build a close relationship with parents, and perform their duties in a culturally competent and responsive manner. They should have an undergraduate or preferably an advanced degree in child development or related field and at least two years of experience in providing the service. Center directors should have supervisory and business experience or training, knowledge of budgeting, knowledge of lesson planning, the ability to train others, and the knowledge to run parent groups.

Role of the Teacher, Family Child Care Home Provider, or Care Provider

In the child care service, the person with the pivotal role in the daily experiences of the child may be called the teacher, family child care home or group child care home provider, or care provider. Regardless of the title or setting, this position requires a special knowledge and understanding of children in addition to skills to enable children to benefit from the child care experience. Teachers/care providers and family child care providers must blend nurturing qualities with the creation of an environment in which children feel comfortable, secure, and protected.

The teacher/care provider or the family child care provider should be a person to whom children can feel close and in whom they feel trust during their time away from home, someone to whom they can turn for help when they need it, and someone from whom they can receive individual attention when they need it.

4.9   Responsibilities of the Teacher/Care Provider in the Center-Based Child Care Program

The child care service should ensure that the teacher/care provider in a center-based child care program participates, as a member of the staff team, in helping individual children and their parents obtain the full benefits of the child care service.

Specific responsibilities of the teacher/care provider include:

- assisting in the initial evaluation of the child's readiness for group experiences and the probable value or limitations of the group for a particular child;
- planning with parents and the director for the preparation of the child to enter the group;
- planning and carrying out the daily developmental learning activities;
- creating an environment that is nurturing, encouraging, culturally competent, and responsive, and that stimulates developmentally appropriate learning;

- ensuring that health, nutrition, and safety practices are observed;
- ensuring that the individual needs of each child are addressed; and
- working in partnership with the parents.

4.10 Responsibilities of the Teacher/Care Provider for Daily Developmental Learning Activities

The child care service should ensure that the teacher/care provider is responsible for developing a daily program of developmental learning and recreational activities that encompass the individual needs of all the children.

The program should be developed in accordance with:

- developmental learning goals and principles;
- current professional knowledge of teaching techniques and curriculum development and content;
- current professional knowledge of social interaction;
- the ages, developmental levels, and interests of each of the children;
- an understanding of the needs and characteristics of the individual children and families participating in the program, including their culture and ethnicity;
- an understanding of child development and culturally and developmentally appropriate activities; and
- an understanding of the health needs of children in general and the special services and equipment required by children with special needs.

4.11 Responsibilities of the Teacher/Care Provider to the Children

The child care service should ensure that the teacher/care provider sees to it that each child obtains a range of learning experiences that promotes development and supplements home experiences.

The teacher/care provider should plan for each child so that:

- as the child arrives, he or she gains a sense of belonging and acceptance in making the transition from home or school;
- the child recognizes that he or she has a particular teacher/care provider on whom to depend for comfort, security, and protection;
- those children having difficulty coping with their environment, with other children, or with the long separation from home and parents receive necessary attention and comfort; and
- before going home, the child is comfortable and appropriately engaged.

4.12 Responsibilities of the Teacher/Care Provider to Parents

The child care service should ensure that from the time of initial enrollment until service termination, the teacher/care provider has a continuing role in daily contact with parents, in individual parent conferences, and in parent group meetings.

The teacher/care provider should:

- recognize that daily contact with parents is one of the most important ways in which parents participate in the child care service;
- discuss daily with the parents their child's progress, problems, and any special events that take place to help the parents understand their child's experience in child care, strengthen the parent-child relationship, and convey to the parents that they are critical in the child's life;
- learn from the parents about the parent-child relationship and those family occurrences that are significant to the child, and share this with any appropriate staff members;
- encourage the parents to visit the child care program at any time when their children are in care;
- maintain records indicating the efforts made to help the child within the program and how the child has progressed;

- be available to offer support to the parents with any difficulties their child may be having and to develop a consistent parent-teacher response (if the child is school age, this effort should be coordinated with the teacher as well); and

- allow sufficient time for teacher/care provider and parent planning when discussing any problems the child may be having.

4.13 Responsibilities of the Teacher/Care Provider in Assessing the Usefulness of the Child Care Experience for the Child During Enrollment and Admission

The child care service should ensure that the teacher/care provider has a major part in evaluating the child's readiness for the child care experience and the probable value or limitations of the particular program for a given child.

Before a child enters a child care program, the teacher/ care provider should have the opportunity to become acquainted with the parents and the child and to observe their relationships and interactions. The teacher/care provider should have information about the child's development, family situation, and any special needs or problems.

The teacher/care provider should plan with the parents how to prepare the child to enter the group.

4.14 Responsibilities of the Teacher/Care Provider in Evaluating the Progress of the Child During the Child Care Experience

The child care service should ensure that the teacher/care provider helps to determine, on the basis of daily interactions with the child, whether the child's experience in the program is in his or her best interests.

The teacher/care provider should help decide when the child is ready for a different care experience (see 4.15) or whether a particular child or parent could benefit from an additional or different type of support.

The teacher/care provider's observations should yield evidence of the ability of each child to benefit from the child care program, the separation from home, and any other problems in the family or the child.

Maintaining accurate, regular records of the child's progress will help to identify any concerns. Evaluations, completed every six months and made available to the parents, should include assessments of the child's development and the extent to which the child is benefiting from the child care experience.

When signs of concerns are noted, the teacher/care provider should give the child the support needed, either directly or by obtaining help from a social worker, mental health consultant, and/or primary health care provider.

4.15 Responsibilities of the Teacher/Care Provider in Determining When a Child Is Ready for Another Experience

The child care service should ensure that the teacher/care provider discusses with the parents and other team members all proposals regarding when a child is ready to leave the particular child care program and transfer to another setting for another experience.

The continuing exchange of information between parents and staff members should help ensure that children will participate in programs most appropriate to their needs.

In determining if a child is ready for another experience, consideration should be given to whether:

- a child has outgrown the activity level of his or her present group and would benefit from a more challenging group; or

- a child is experiencing difficulties within the setting and could benefit from another, perhaps smaller or more specialized, setting.

Determining if a child needs another experience should never be based on funding issues.

Teachers/care providers should be responsible for preparing the parent and the child for the new experience.

4.16 Role of the Teacher/Care Provider as a Member of the Child Care Service Team

The child care service should expect the teacher/care provider to work with and learn from other staff members and to contribute his or her understanding of a particular child to the other members of the team. The teacher/care provider should contribute concepts regarding how children learn, how individual children differ at different ages and stages of development, and how the developmental learning experiences of the child care program can best meet the individual needs of children.

4.17 Skills Required by the Teacher/Care Provider

Lead teachers/care providers should possess a bachelor's degree in early childhood education, child development, or a related field, plus at least one year of experience working in a child care setting. Assistant teachers/care providers should have an associate degree in early childhood development, child development, or a related field, or a child development associate (CDA) certification or equivalent education and training certification. All teachers should be cardiopulmonary resuscitation (CPR) and first-aid certified and should participate in annual training and professional development opportunities. Lead teachers, as well as assistant teachers, should be culturally competent.

In addition, all teaching staff should:

- like and understand children,
- offer children affection and security,
- find satisfaction in caring for children,
- be able to create a favorable atmosphere for children,
- have the personal characteristics that will supply continuity of care throughout the child's need for care,
- meet the common needs of children,
- be comfortable caring for children with special needs, and

• be able to handle an emergency promptly and intelligently.

4.18 Special Skills Required by the Teacher/Care Provider of Infants or Toddlers

Teachers/care providers working with infants and toddlers should have additional skills and personality traits in order to effectively work with this age group. They should be able to bathe, feed, change, hold, and comfort infants. In addition, they should be able to calm the infant, help with transitions in the infants' daily schedule, and provide quick responses to the needs of the infants and toddlers in their care.

Persons working with this age group should be caring and patient.

4.19 Responsibilities of Child Care Aides

The child care service should ensure that the responsibilities of child care aides include assisting the lead teacher and the assistant teacher in program activities, supervising play activities as requested, and observing and reporting on children's behavior.

4.20 Skills Required of Child Care Aides

Child care aides should have a high school diploma or GED certificate, be literate in a language, and should demonstrate an investment in learning about child development and child care services.

4.21 Responsibilities of Child Care Student Interns/ Volunteers

The child care service should ensure that child care student interns or volunteers assist teachers/care providers and child care aides on a part-time basis, under supervision.

4.22 Skills Required by Student Interns/Volunteers

The student intern/volunteer should be currently enrolled in a high school or college child care course and should demonstrate an investment in learning about child development and child care services.

4.23 Responsibilities of the Provider in a Family Child Care/Group Child Care Home

The family child care provider should ensure that individual children and their parents obtain the full benefits of the child care service.

The responsibilities of the family child care home/group home provider should be the same as all responsibilities of teachers/care providers in center-based programs (see 4.9–4.15).

Family child care/group child care providers can be independent or part of a family child care network/system. Providers in a network/system should have additional responsibilities related to the system and should receive additional services in return (see Chapter 6, Family Child Care Networks/Systems).

Specific responsibilities of the family child care provider include:

- assisting in the initial evaluation of the child's readiness for group experiences and the probable value or limitations of the group for a particular child;
- planning with parents for the preparation of the child to enter the group;
- planning and carrying out the daily developmental learning activities;
- creating an environment that is nurturing, encouraging, and culturally competent, and that stimulates developmentally appropriate learning;
- ensuring that health, nutrition, and safety practices are observed;
- ensuring that the individual needs of each child are addressed; and
- working in partnership with the parents.

4.24 Responsibilities of the Provider in a Family Child Care/Group Child Care Home for Daily Developmental Learning Activities

The family child care provider should be responsible for developing a daily program of developmental learning and recreational activities that can encompass individual needs of all the children.

The program should be developed in accordance with:

- developmental learning goals and principles;
- current professional knowledge of teaching techniques and curriculum development and content;
- current professional knowledge of social interaction;
- the ages, maturity levels, and interests of each of the children;
- an understanding of the needs and characteristics of the individual children and families participating in the program, including their culture and ethnicity;
- an understanding of child development and culturally and developmentally appropriate activities; and
- an understanding of the health needs of children in general and for specific children, including the special services and equipment required by children with special needs.

4.25 Responsibilities of the Provider in a Family Child Care/Group Child Care Home to the Children

The family child care provider should see to it that each child obtains a range of learning experiences that promotes development and supplements home experiences.

The provider should plan for each child so that:

- as the child arrives, he or she gains a sense of belonging and acceptance in making the transition from home or school;
- the child recognizes that he or she can depend on the family child care provider for comfort, security, and protection;
- those children having difficulty coping with their environment, with other children, or with the long sepa-

ration from home and parents receive necessary attention and comfort; and

- before going home, the child is comfortable and appropriately engaged.

4.26 Responsibilities of the Provider in a Family Child Care/Group Child Care Home to the Parents

The family child care provider should ensure that from the time
of initial enrollment until the termination of service, he or she
has a continuing role in daily contact with parents, in individual parent conferences, and in parent group meetings.

The family child care provider should:

- recognize that daily contact with parents is one of
the most important ways in which parents participate in the child care service;
- discuss daily with the parents the child's progress,
problems, and any special events that take place to
help parents understand their child's experience in
child care, strengthen parent-child relationships, and
convey to parents that they are critical in the child's
life;
- learn from parents about the parent-child relationship
and those family occurrences that are significant to
the child, and share this with any appropriate staff
members;
- encourage parents to visit the family child care home
at any time when their children are in care;
- maintain records indicating the efforts made to help
the child within the program and how the child has
progressed;
- be available to offer support to parents with any difficulties a child may be having and to develop consistent parent-teacher response (if the child is school
age, this effort should be coordinated with the teacher
as well); and
- allow sufficient time for family child care provider-
parent planning when discussing any problems the
child may be having.

4.27 Responsibilities of the Provider in a Family Child Care/Group Child Care Home in Assessing the Usefulness of the Child Care Experience for the Child During Enrollment and Admission

The family child care provider should ensure that evaluating the child's readiness for the child care experience and the probable values or limitations of the particular program for a given child is a major part of the enrollment process.

Before a child enters a child care program, the family child care provider should have the opportunity to become acquainted with the parents and the child and to observe their relationships and interactions. The family child care provider should have information about the child's development, family situation, and any special needs or problems.

The family child care provider should plan with the parents how to prepare the child to enter the group.

4.28 Responsibilities of the Provider in a Family Child Care/Group Child Care Home in Evaluating the Progress of the Child During the Child Care Experience

The family child care provider should determine, on the basis of daily interactions with the child, whether the child's experience in the program is in his or her best interests.

The family child care provider should help decide when the child is ready for a different care experience or whether a particular child or parent could benefit from an additional or different type of support.

The family child care provider's observations should yield evidence of the ability of each child to benefit from the child care program, the separation from home, and any other problems in the family or the child.

Maintaining accurate, regular records of the child's progress will help to identify any concerns. Evaluations, completed every six months and made available to the parents, should include assessments of the child's development and the extent to which the child is benefiting from the child care experience.

When signs of concerns are noted, the family child care provider should give the child the support needed, either directly or by obtaining help from a social worker, mental health consultant, and/or primary health care provider.

4.29 Responsibilities of the Provider in a Family Child Care/Group Child Care Home in Determining When a Child Is Ready for Another Experience

The family child care provider should discuss with the parents all proposals regarding when a child is ready to leave the particular child care program and transfer to another setting for another experience.

The continuing exchange of information between parents and providers should help ensure that children will participate in programs most appropriate to their needs.

In determining if a child is ready for another experience, consideration should be given to whether:

- a child has outgrown the activity level of his or her present group and would benefit from a more challenging group; or
- a child is experiencing difficulties within the setting and could benefit from another, perhaps smaller or more specialized, setting.

Determining if a child needs another experience should never be based on funding issues.

Family child care providers should be responsible for preparing the parent and the child for the new experience.

4.30 Skills Required by Family and Group Home Child Care Providers

The child care service should ensure that family child care providers and group home child care providers participate in 40 hours of training annually.

In addition, family child care providers should:

- have at least a high school diploma or GED and have had at least 90 hours of training in business management, health and safety, nutrition, child development, child abuse and neglect, working with children with special needs, behavior management; and parent relationships;

• like and understand children;

• offer children affection and security;

• be culturally competent;

• find satisfaction in caring for children;

• create a favorable atmosphere for children;

• have the personal characteristics that will supply continuity of care throughout the child's need for care;

• meet the common needs of children;

• be comfortable caring for children with special needs;

• be mature (at least 21 years old), with the energy and flexibility necessary to care for young children and their changing needs;

• be able to handle an emergency promptly and intelligently;

• be in good health, as evidenced by a physical examination of each member of the family certifying (1) freedom from physical or mental illness, (2) the absence of a communicable disease or condition, and (3) no involvement with alcohol or drug abuse by any family member; and

• have no conviction for a crime involving child neglect or abuse, alcohol, or illegal chemical substances.

4.31   Use of Consultants

The child care service should provide staff members and parents with access to medical, mental health, nutrition, and social services, using consultants to complement staff members' capabilities.

The child care service should ensure access to consultants depending on the size and complexity of the child care service and the resources available.

4.32 Integration of All Components of the Child Care Service

The director of the agency of which the child care service is a part is responsible for integrating all service components of the agency so children and their parents experience the service as a single, comprehensive program.

The director is responsible for helping staff members, parents, and the community better understand ways in which the knowledge and skills of different professional groups can best be used in maintaining an effective child care service.

Staff Recruitment and Selection

4.33 Plan for Staff Recruitment

The child care service should have a plan for the ongoing recruitment of all the types of staff needed to provide services.

The staff recruitment process may include the following:

- recruiting based on recommendations of current staff members;
- distributing brochures/flyers describing the services;
- advertising in local media;
- establishing a speakers bureau;
- establishing relationships with local business, civic, religious, cultural, and social groups or other human service agencies; and
- contacting and developing relationships with staff training and research personnel in child development associate programs, colleges, and other educational settings.

4.34 Screening and Selecting Staff Members

The child care service should ensure that supervisors screen and select candidates for employment on the basis of each applicant's education, training, personal qualities, experiences, cultural competencies, and potential for developing the attitudes and skills necessary to carry out the responsibilities of the given position.

The selection process should include:

- visits and interviews during which the applicant can learn about the children and families served, services provided, job requirements, benefits, training programs, and qualifications needed for the job;

- an initial comprehensive health examination as protection to the applicant and the children and families served;

- references obtained from previous employers and personal friends; and

- criminal background checks with law enforcement agencies and the child abuse information systems.

Although screening for criminal and child abuse records is critical to the hiring of staff members for work with children, and is mandated in most jurisdictions, it is important to note that child abuse registry information is not universally available to all child care services. Furthermore, state and local law enforcement agencies often have difficulty providing accurate and complete information in a timely manner.

In addition to checking with available government information sources, the child care service should rely on its own references and interviews.

4.35 Cultural Diversity and Competence of Staff

The child care service should be committed to establishing and maintaining a culturally diverse work force and becoming a culturally competent organization.

The families served by the child care service are racially and culturally diverse, and the service should reflect that diversity. The child care service should recruit and hire staff who are culturally diverse and sensitive to the expressed needs of the populations served.

To successfully recruit staff members representative of diverse racial and cultural groups, the child care service, depending on the size and type of program, should:

- make a conscious commitment to recruit and hire staff members from those groups served by the community;

- develop a positive relationship with the communities served;
- ask community members for specific assistance in recruitment;
- develop relationships with schools of education, social work, or other professions, encouraging students who come from the community to use the agency as a site for field placements;
- consider bilingual and bicultural competency in addition to formal training and experience in evaluating the qualifications of professionals and paraprofessionals; and
- establish a staff development program that includes career advancement policies and mentoring and that provides opportunities for staff members from diverse groups to prepare for and assume supervisory and administrative positions.

To retain staff members from diverse cultural groups, the agency must demonstrate cultural responsiveness to all staff members as well as to the children and families it serves.

The agency should ensure that staff members at every level, as well as members of governing or advisory boards, are representative of the populations being served.

Orientation, Training, and Staff Development

The child care service should provide opportunities for professional growth and development for all staff members by means of orientation, inservice training, supervision, staff development programs, and educational leave, as well as staff participation in the development of agency policies. The program should be planned and provided in collaboration with experienced practitioners and—where appropriate—with health care professionals, substance abuse specialists, family violence specialists, child development specialists, early childhood educators, and advocates. Training should model the value and practice of teamwork. The training program should incorporate new practice developments and reflect best practice in the field.

4.36 Competency-Based Staff Development

Management should clearly define the qualifications and competencies required of all staff.

Competency is defined as the qualifications, skills, and knowledge required to meet performance standards. Competency also includes the demonstration of behavior, personal characteristics, and interpersonal problem solving skills that are necessary to be effective in the position. Competency may be measured by direct observation of required skills, successful completion of required training, demonstration of knowledge of relevant policies and procedures, and successful completion of objective testing instruments.

Specific competencies should be established in every service area. Core competencies should be identified and staff should be assessed based on those competencies. The assessment of core competencies should include, at a minimum, verification by review of work products and direct observation.

Direct care competencies should include the following:
- developmentally appropriate learning practices;
- classroom management;
- age-appropriate curriculum development;
- effective communication;
- development of healthy relationships;
- maintaining a healthy, safe, and secure work environment;
- maintaining a healthy, safe, and clean learning setting;
- protecting children from maltreatment;
- fostering equality, diversity, and rights;
- knowing age- and population-specific competencies;
- preparing food and drink;
- receiving, transmitting, and retrieving information;

- administering medication; and
- working with children with special needs.

4.37 Staff Development and Training Personnel

The child care service should assign qualified staff members to organize and carry out a staff development and training program. All staff members and others who lead training should be prepared as trainers, have skills in working with groups, and have a thorough understanding of the program content.

All persons providing training should have knowledge of the following:

- the purpose, goals, philosophy, and organizational structure of the child care service, the agency it is part of, if applicable, and the relationship of the child care service to other services in the community;
- agency requirements and expectations relating to monitoring and supervision;
- the roles, rights, and responsibilities of parents, the child, and the agency;
- health and safety procedures; and
- the ethnic and cultural environments of the service area.

The child care service should provide the necessary resources and administrative support to the staff development and training program to ensure success.

Staff development personnel should have adequate resources in technology, audiovisual supplies, training equipment, and meeting space.

4.38 Responsibility for Staff Development and Training

Staff development responsibilities should include but not be limited to formulating and disseminating an agency staff development plan; tracking, monitoring, and documenting staff involvement in staff development activities; recommending policies for continuing education opportunities and educational leave; gathering and disseminating information on staff development activities; ensuring access to materials; maintaining information on the code of ethics for various professional disciplines; and evaluating and making needed revisions to training.

The agency staff development plan should provide continuing education unit requirements for specific staff positions; specify training requirements consistent with licensing and accreditation standards; allow for input from all agency staff members, youth, and families served; and incorporate training needs as determined by performance evaluations of staff members.

Access to materials may be provided through an onsite library, Internet access, and other resources to enhance staff training and development experiences.

4.39 Staff Orientation

The child care service supervisor should give all new staff members an orientation to the agency and the child care service as an initial component of a staff development program.

The orientation should focus on the staff member's role in the child care service, and enable the new staff member to increase both knowledge and understanding of the needs of children and their parents.

4.40 Content of Staff Orientation

The child care service should ensure that staff members receive an agency-specific orientation before being assigned to work with children and their families. If new staff members come without specific job qualifications, the agency should consider providing training to eliminate any deficits.

The orientation should include:

- an introduction to the agency and the child care service;
- an introduction to the program's goals, philosophy, and the new staff member's job description;
- the cultures of the children and families served;
- the special needs of the children and families served;

- state and local child abuse and neglect reporting requirements, and the child care service's reporting policies and procedures on suspected child abuse and neglect;
- articulation of the role of each member of the child care service team; and
- an introduction to the demographics of the children and families served.

4.41 Inservice Training

The child care service should ensure that staff members receive inservice training throughout their employment with the agency.

Each new staff member should have an individual training plan that includes an assessment of his or her educational and training needs and interests and a systematic plan to develop the needed competencies.

Regular inservice training should address:

- child development, with an emphasis on the developmental stages of the child;
- information on community and cultural resources;
- values and principles of child welfare and child care practices;
- practice in identifying the strengths and needs of children and their families, and how best to achieve the goals of service;
- components of age-appropriate daily programs;
- characteristics of helping relationships with parents and other staff members;
- child abuse and neglect statutes and the child care staff member's responsibility for reporting suspected cases;
- the causes, signs, symptoms, and treatment of child abuse and neglect;
- recognizing risk and protective factors to build resiliency for children;
- trauma and its impact, including exposure to violence in the home, the community, and the media;

- practical implications of cultural and ethnic differences;
- stresses on low-income families, including the effects of poverty on family members and their relationships;
- effective communication styles and techniques;
- first aid, CPR, and administering medication;
- licensing and regulations;
- identification of possible health problems and appropriate program protocols;
- confidentiality policy; and
- emergency procedures.

4.42 Characteristics of Inservice Training

The child care service should ensure that training for all staff members of the child care service has an experiential and situational emphasis, rather than an exclusively didactic approach. All staff members of the child care service should receive at least 40 hours of training each year as a means to achieve required competencies.

A competency-based training curriculum, highlighting skills to match job responsibilities, is recommended.

The training should be evaluated using measurable outcomes.

4.43 Inservice Training for Supervisors

The child care service should ensure that all staff in supervisory positions receive inservice training throughout their employment with the agency.

Each supervisor should have an individual training plan that includes an assessment of their educational and training needs and interests and a systematic plan to develop the needed competencies.

The inservice training should be competency based with identified learning outcomes, and should, depending upon the size and type of service provided, reflect a combination of modalities, including:

- didactic training with practice and role plays;
- reading and discussion of program manuals, guidelines, and relevant articles;

- assignment of a peer mentor for ongoing support and discussion;
- ongoing, regular supervision;
- ongoing, periodic training sessions; and
- opportunities for self-reflection and self-evaluation.

Training should include, but not be limited to:

- review of the mission, values, and treatment philosophy of the child care service and the agency it is part of, if applicable, and of the supervisor's role in creating an agency culture that promotes them;
- clarification of supervisory job duties and responsibilities;
- review of personnel policies and issues in implementation;
- the supervisor as a manager, model for staff, and leader;
- building and leading a cohesive team;
- boundary issues for supervisors promoted from within;
- conducting effective staff meetings;
- conducting effective individual and group supervision sessions with staff;
- strategies for supporting the growth and development of staff members;
- review of supervisor's role in the service planning and review process;
- consulting with staff on child-related issues;
- monitoring and evaluating staff performance;
- working with challenging staff members;
- quality improvement and program evaluation guidelines and procedures;
- cultural competence;
- selecting, hiring, and training staff;
- knowledge of applicable federal and state laws and their intent; and

- enlisting the support of management, other agency programs, and the community in strengthening services and creating a supportive environment for staff.

4.44 Other Required Training

The child care service should encourage staff members to obtain additional hours of training each year.

These training experiences could include:

- participating in peer support meetings led by a child care service supervisor;

- attending local, regional, or national conferences on child care, child development, or related child welfare issues;

- reading professional literature, completing self-instructional workbooks, or viewing relevant audiovisual materials;

- participating in groups sessions with staff consultants;

- participating in community classes, such as those offered by the American Red Cross, Visiting Nurses Association, parent and adult education programs, or university extension courses; and

- augmenting formal training with on-the-job supervision, job rotation, access to professional consultation, and self-directed training.

4.45 Probationary Period

The child care service should evaluate the status of the child care staff member after he or she has successfully completed the orientation program and a probationary period that includes observation of the new staff member's work with children and families.

The results of the orientation program and the observed practice experience should enable the new staff member and supervisor to determine whether the staff member's interests, qualifications, and skills match the requirements for the position.

4.46 Policy Regarding Substance Abuse by Employees

To reduce the risk of agency liability and safeguard both the children in its care and its staff members, the child care service should examine all relevant state and local laws, regulations, and insurance conditions to guide the development of its substance abuse policies.

Careful staff screening by means of reference checks with previous employers, criminal records, or substance abuse history, and clear documentation of pre-employment guidelines with respect to a drug-free workplace should precede but not substitute for, preservice and inservice staff training.

4.47 Salaries

The child care service should ensure that salaries for all staff members of the child care service are sufficient to attract people with the qualifications for performing the duties of the position, and they should be comparable to those paid in the community for other positions of equal responsibility.

The child care service should accept responsibility for advocating for appropriate staff salaries within the community, as well as within the state and nationwide.

Family and group care providers should receive remuneration equivalent to their responsibilities and qualifications.

4.48 Benefits

The child care service should provide a full range of benefits for all its employees, with particular attention to sick leave and health insurance.

Among the other benefits that should be considered are annual leave, a retirement program, personal days, flex time, dental coverage, disability insurance, an employee assistance program, and child care for employees.

4.49 Staff Supervision

The child care service should provide supervision for all staff members to promote both the recruitment and the retention of highly qualified, experienced personnel. To assure adequate attention to the needs of both the staff members providing care and the children in their care, a supervisor should directly supervise no more than six staff members. All child care service members should receive formal supervision or monitoring at least once a week.

Supervisors should be available, as necessary, for consultation with those employees under their supervision.

Supervisors should review children's records periodically to assure the provision of quality practices. Both specialized and informal supervision should also be made available to staff members to help them in assessing, planning for, and working with children and families who have multiple and complex concerns.

Supervisors and consultants should be available to accompany staff members on home visits to assist in assessing the family and/or providing services.

4.50 Career Ladder

The child care service should develop a career ladder for all of its employees that offers both horizontal and vertical opportunities for advancement and benefits commensurate with increased experience, skills, and/or responsibilities.

The career ladder should be developed based on the child care service's professional development plans for the entire program staff and individual staff members. The plan should demonstrate the service's expectations for and commitment to a highly trained, skilled, and qualified workforce.

The retention of qualified and experienced staff members should be a goal of the child care service. Toward this end, the child care service should create a work environment conducive to relieving stress and supportive of staff members. Emphasis should be placed on supporting staff members through expert consultation, attendance at professional conferences and seminars, and recognition of outstanding performance.

4.51 Creating a Supportive Work Environment

The child care service should create a work environment that is supportive to all of its staff members.

A supportive work environment helps to prevent worker burnout and turnover, and increases job productivity and satisfaction (CWLA, 2001; U.S. GAO, 2003). A supportive work environment should include:

- valuing employees as individuals and for the unique contributions they bring to the program and the children and families served;
- recognizing the personal and professional needs of each employee;
- encouraging employees to work as a team and to support one another toward common goals;
- creating an environment free from harassment and workplace violence;
- supporting employees when they ask for help and assistance;
- exhibiting confidence in staff members;
- creating a climate of trust and open communication;
- being sensitive to staff members' potential history of trauma;
- being receptive and responsive to employee concerns and suggestions;
- supporting staff members through training and other experiences related to improving professional growth;
- providing regular guidance and supervision;
- allowing employees to participate in the setting of their own goals;
- rewarding accomplishments, responsibility, initiative, and creativity;
- providing opportunities for employees to contribute to decisions that affect the agency, its personnel, and the children they serve;
- providing personnel policies and procedures that are fair and honest and that facilitate the building of supportive relationships among the members of the staff;

- providing access to employee assistance programs such as counseling and substance abuse services;
- establishing and providing training and assistance to staff regarding sexual harassment and workplace violence; and
- providing supportive benefits such as family leave.

In addition to creating a supportive work environment, the residential service agency should create an atmosphere that is culturally supportive of all staff. This includes:

- acknowledging, respecting, and embracing different points of view in the workplace;
- specifying cultural competence and responsiveness in all job descriptions and including attention to these qualities in performance evaluations;
- establishing personnel policies that are supportive and responsive to all staff members;
- asking community members to assist in identifying additional factors that will create a supportive environment;
- providing leave-time policies that accommodate holidays and important community or family events of the various cultures represented by staff members;
- in evaluating agency performance, asking consumers from the community for their perceptions of the agency's effectiveness;
- using agency decor that reflects diversity;
- incorporating training on relevant child welfare law and policy, including ICWA;
- helping raise sensitivity and awareness of community members to the diversity of their communities, including tribal communities, to encourage support of and decrease isolation among community members; and
- celebrating and sharing cultural backgrounds, traditions, and practices within the organization.

Staff training curricula should include a focus on building staff members' cultural competence and increasing their understanding of the role of culture in a person's life.

The agency should build relationships with community representatives who can orient staff members to the values and beliefs, customs, needs, strengths, and resources of the community and its culture. The agency should seek information from these communities and incorporate that information as appropriate throughout the family service system.

Size and Groupings of Child Care Programs

4.52 Size of the Child Care Service

The child care service determines the total number of children cared for by using such considerations as the need within the community, the physical facilities, the availability of family and group care homes, the age of the children, staffing, administrative structure, travel distances, and transportation resources.

In very small centers that provide care for only one or two groups of children, it may be difficult to provide a diversified program with stimulation and adequate staff development. Also, per capita administrative costs may be very high. These difficulties may be minimized if several small centers are operated under one administrative center or become part of a coordinated community child care program.

A single unit of one group of children served in a family or group child care home may realize substantial benefits and program enhancements if it is included as part of a child care network operated by either a center or an agency (see Chapter 6, Family Child Care Networks/Systems).

4.53 Ages and Numbers of Children in Each Child Care Program

The child care service should be aware that the ages and numbers of children in each child care program, and the ratio of adults to children, are important determinants of the quality of the child care experience for the child.

Generally, children should be grouped according to age. Studies are beginning to show, however, that under certain circumstances, mixed-age groupings may be beneficial to the development of children and to fulfill other specific purposes (see Introduction, p. 30).

4.54 Group Size and Teacher-Child Ratio

The child care services should base the number of children enrolled in a child care service group on the age of the children.

A significant body of research relates quality in child care with group size and shows that group size is the most consistent factor in determining quality of care. In addition, lower teacher-child ratios were also related to the quality of care, with the smallest ratios creating the highest quality. (Peisner-Feinberg et al., 1999). Smaller groups are consistently found to be the most effective in center, group child care homes, and family child care homes. The following group sizes and teacher-child ratios are recommended:

Age of Children	Max. # of Children in Group	Teacher/Care Provider–Child Ratio
Birth to 12 months	6	1:3
13 to 24 months	8	1:4
25 to 36 months	10	1:5
37 to 48 months	14	1:7
Maximum group size	20	1:10

The staffing ratios assume attention to appropriate staffing patterns and consistent caregivers. Hiring fewer trained caregivers or counting auxiliary personnel to meet staff-child ratios is not recommended. In addition, every effort should be made to provide each child and group of children with a primary caregiver who does not change. This continuity of care has been shown to increase the quality of care for all children.

4.55 Principles of Grouping Children

The child care service should ensure that each age grouping allows for a three-month variance, depending on the best interests of the children in the particular group.

Children should be grouped so as to allow for:

- protection of younger children from the behavior of older children;
- differences in the interests, attention spans, and physical and intellectual maturity of younger and older children;
- differences in developmental maturity of children of the same chronological age;
- appropriate expectations for all children; and
- opportunities for periodic association with children of other ages.

4.56 Staffing Requirements for Infants

The child care service should ensure that in the group of infants, at least one primary caregiver should be with the children at all times, and there should be no more than three infants to each adult caregiver when separate units are used. In family care homes, one infant per caregiver is preferred, but no more than two children under the age of 2 years, including the child of the family care provider.

When more than two infants are cared for in a family care home, the home should meet the same staff ratios as a center. For any mixed age groupings with children younger than 3, the teacher/care provider-child ratio for the youngest child should be followed.

4.57 Group Size for Physically and Emotionally Challenged Children

The child care service should ensure that group sizes in child care programs established to care exclusively for physically challenged children or those with emotional disabilities are smaller than the sizes recommended for general programs to ensure care in accordance with the needs of the children.

4.58 Number of Children in Family Child Care Homes

The child care service should ensure that the family child care home is used for no more that six children younger than 14 years of age, including those children of the family care provider who will be in the home during the hours of care. No more than two children younger than 2 years of age should be in the care of the family care provider, including those of the care provider, should be care for in the home.

The specific number and ages of children who should be served in a family child care home, including those of the family care provider (up to the recommended staff-child ratios), should be determined by the physical strength, skills, and capacity of the family care provider.

The provider's ability to serve children of different ages and the physical accommodations of the home should be considered when determining the number of children allowed in care.

4.59 Number of Children in Group Child Care Homes

The child care service should ensure that the group child care home is used for no more than 12 children younger than the age of 14, including the children of the provider(s) who will be in the home during the hours of care.

The specific number and ages of children who should be served in a group care home, including those of the group child care provider, should be determined by the physical strength, skills, and capacities of the group care provider.

The provider's ability to serve children of different ages and the physical accommodations of the home should be considered when determining the number of children allowed in care.

5

Organization and Administration of the Child Care Service

Goals

I. The policies, procedures, and practice of the child care service ensure that quality, culturally competent services are provided to children and families and that all legal requirements are met.

II. The child care service develops, maintains, and updates policies, procedures, and outcomes that direct the delivery of services to children and families and that are readily available to staff and the community.

III. The child care service staff have the resources, training, education, competencies, commitment, workload, and administrative support needed to help children, families, and the program achieve desired outcomes.

IV. The child care service hires, retains, and develops competent, qualified, diverse staff to administer, manage, and deliver culturally competent child care and education services.

V. The child care service provides children and families with access to child care and education services

155

that are developmentally appropriate, coordinated, culturally competent, and of high quality.

VI. The child care service involves families in the design, delivery, oversight, and evaluation of its programs and services.

VII. The information management system maintained by the child care service captures the information that is important to child care service delivery, including tracking data on children and families, program evaluation, and fiscal management.

VIII. The information collected by the child care service is used to evaluate the child care services, improve service delivery, and advocate for sufficient staff, fiscal support, and resources.

IX. The child care service receives feedback from consumers, community, parents and children, staff, and board members (as applicable) through formal processes such as surveys and focus groups.

CWLA's *Standards of Excellence for the Management and Governance of Child Welfare Organizations* (1996) present the management and governance components of child welfare practice that apply across the field. It is intended to serve as the primary source on organization and management for all CWLA program standards. This chapter expands upon some of the content of those standards to highlight aspects of organization and management that are particularly germane to delivering quality child care, development, and education services.

Basic Responsibilities

5.1   Authorization

The agency administering the child care service should be authorized by law to serve children outside their own homes for a portion of the day.

Any public agency administering a child care service should be expected to meet the same standards of care as those established for voluntary agencies having the same service.

Not-for-profit and for-profit agencies offering child care services should operate in accordance with a charter and by-laws, and be monitored under state or local regulations. They should meet the requirements of the appropriate state department or tribal council and be licensed for child care service.

The agency should meet minimum standards for size and specifications of facilities, qualifications, required number of staff members, program or curriculum content, child-staff ratios, and maximum group and center size, as set by local and state jurisdictions.

5.2   Provision of Service by Public Agencies

The public agency responsible for child care may do so either by offering the services directly or by purchasing the service from other agencies or providers.

A variety of agencies may have responsibility for child care.

5.3   Composition and Responsibilities of the Advisory Board of the Public Agency

The advisory board of the public agency providing the child care service should reflect the diversity of the cultural and ethnic groups in the community served. The board is responsible for staying informed about the service, for making appropriate recommendations to the administrative authority when service changes or new policies are needed, for obtaining input from representatives of the community, and for ensuring quality standards for the child care service.

5.4   Composition and Responsibilities of the Private Agency Board of Directors

The board of directors of the private agency providing the child care service should reflect the diversity of the cultural and ethnic groups in the community served; provide a variety of experience, expertise, and guidance to the agency; be composed of individuals who receive no compensation for services; operate as its governing body; and determine that the services provided are responsive to the needs of children and families in the community served.

The private agency board should be responsible for:

- defining the purpose, goals, and scope of the agency program in relation to community needs and the population served;
- developing and approving policies to direct the service;
- establishing and maintaining a sound financial structure and ensuring financial support and staffing for the agency's purpose and programs;
- building community understanding and support for the services provided; and
- determining that the agency fulfills its purpose and responsibilities.

The private agency board of directors should employ a professionally qualified and competent director to administer the child care service in accord with its policies. It should develop and promulgate policies for the child care service to properly carry out its functions.

The governing board should have a clear understanding of its role and the partnership it has with the child care service staff and the parents using the service.

The board is accountable to the community it serves. As such, it should advocate for children and families who need child care services and evaluate the programs in relation to the changing needs of the community.

5.5   Responsibilities of the Public Agency

The public agency should license private agencies to provide child care, development, and education services to children and their families; set and maintain minimum care and protection requirements; offer consultation in the development of policies, procedures, and organizational guidance to support quality service delivery; and withhold licensing from those agencies that do not meet the licensing requirements. If the public agency administers its own services, it should be expected to maintain the same standards required of any service provider.

5.6   Responsibilities of the Private Agency

The private agency providing child care, development, and education services should determine the needs of the children and families served, provide services in accordance with quality standards, and assist families in obtaining additional services from other agencies in the community as needed by them.

5.7   Provision of Service by a Single Service or Multiservice Agency

The child care service operated by an agency may be one of several services offered for children and families, or it may be the agency's sole program.

5.8   Child Care Service Manual

The child care service should write the policies and procedures governing the service in a consistent format and organize them in an agency manual available for use by staff members, parents, and cooperating community agencies. The contents of the manual should give staff members a clear statement of their roles and responsibilities.

A copy of the manual should be given to all staff members when they begin their employment and be on hand for ready use as a resource. Introduction to the manual should be a part of the child care service's staff orientation program.

The manual should be available in hard copy (paper) as well as electronically and should include a system for timely updating and distribution of new policies.

A separate manual may be prepared exclusively for use by parents.

5.9   Child Care Records

The child care service should maintain a service record for each child receiving services, from the time of application and admission to termination of the child care services. The child care record for each child should contain a current and continuing account of the nature of the center's or home's involvement with the child and an assessment of the child's development.

Records should be available and accessible to teachers and care providers at all times, even during field trips or emergency relocations. Records should comply with federal and state regulations regarding access to information and confidentiality, and should include, for each child, the following information:

- child name, address, gender, and date of birth;
- names of custodial parents and their home and work addresses and telephone numbers;
- names, addresses, and telephone numbers of two additional persons to be notified if parents cannot be reached;
- names, addresses, and telephone numbers of the child's primary health care provider and dentist, or preferred medical and dental care facility;
- basic health information, including immunization records, developmental status, description of any physical, sensory, or emotional problems, any allergies, and any special treatment/attention required;
- signed authorizations for transportation, emergency care, field trips, release of child to anyone other than the custodial parent, and release of any information to schools or other agencies; and
- signed statements, in the language that the parents most commonly use, that the parents have received copies of the state's child abuse reporting requirements, and the center's or home's policies with respect to behavior management, emergency procedures, sick children, and payment requirements.

The record should include initial and periodic assessment of the child's development based on a child care service plan developed by the child's parents and the care provider. In addition, the record should include any notable observations by care providers with respect to the child and the family and accounts of parent conferences and significant activities and communications.

A periodic review of each child's record and a summary of progress made should be used for evaluations by the supervisory and administrative staff. These summaries should be written in a consistent agency format developed in collaboration with staff members.

5.10 Confidentiality of Records

All child care records are confidential and should be maintained in locked file cabinets or other secure settings. Access to written records should be subject to clear, written agency procedures.

Abuses of this privacy policy should lead to appropriate disciplinary action.

The child care service should retain the record on each child until he or she reaches the age of 21.

Policies

5.11 Policy on Corporal Punishment

The child care service should have a clear policy prohibiting corporal punishment.

Corporal punishment is the infliction of physical pain for the purpose of discipline.

The following actions should be prohibited:

- slapping, spanking, paddling, or belting the child;
- forcing the child to march, stand, or kneel rigidly in one spot;
- humiliating the child, using oral abuse, depriving the child of meals, or force feeding the child; and
- disciplining the child for soiling, wetting, or not using the toilet.

Many methods of discipline are more effective and safer than corporal punishment. All child-serving agencies, including the child care service, should advocate for the prohibition of corporal punishment.

5.12 Policy on Behavioral Guidance

The child care service should have a concrete policy on behavioral guidance that emphasizes the acceptance of each child as a valuable member of society, to be treated with dignity and respect at all times.

The primary goals of a behavioral guidance policy should be to teach each child to build self-regulation and to keep all children in the program safe.

5.13 Prevention Strategies

The child care service should have a behavioral guidance policy with clear, useful prevention strategies. Child care providers should take active steps in preventing problem behaviors and all staff should be trained in these prevention strategies.

Through simple planning and preparation, child care services can prevent negative behavior before it happens.

The prevention strategies should include:

- planned daily routines that provide structure, but also offer flexibility for the individual needs of the child, including cultural differences;
- appropriate behavior modeled by adults in the service;
- clearly stated/demonstrated expectations and goals;
- strong, supportive relationships between child and care provider;
- positive reinforcement of appropriate behavior;
- logical alternatives and redirection of children towards more positive behavior; and
- using guest experts or consultants to discuss developmental behavior and management of behavioral challenges with staff and children.

5.14 Intervention

The child care service should ensure that when prevention strategies fail and children exhibit problem behaviors that interrupt the classroom and place themselves or others in danger, child care providers are ready to intervene with appropriate, predetermined measures.

Intervention policies should include:

- recognizing the child's feelings and helping him or her to understand that the behavior is unacceptable;
- helping the child to identify the consequences of his or her behavior;
- offering the child a quiet, supervised space to regain control with the goal of rejoining the group; and
- clearly restating the rules and expectations.

5.15 Emergency Situations (Supportive Holding)

When a child poses an immediate, serious threat to his or her own safety, or the safety of other members of the group or the surrounding environment, the child care service should permit the teacher/care provider to use supportive holding/physical restraint.

Physical restraint involves actions taken by the care provider to control the child's movement and actions to guide the child in becoming more compliant. Situations in which supportive holding is permitted should be clearly stated in the child care program's behavioral guidance policy.

The child care provider may only hold the child long enough to protect him or her from the dangerous situation and return the child to safety. Supportive holding is to be used only as a last resort, not as a discipline technique.

Touch is key to the positive development of children. Touch should also be used as positive reinforcement in the forms of hugs, holding a child's hand, or the like. When touch is used only in supportive holding, children will tend to associate touch with only a negative, punitive response.

5.16 Follow-Up on Behavioral Incidents

The child care service should ensure that behavioral incidents are followed up with a process of evaluation and communication.

This process may include documentation of the incident, communication with the parents or guardians and other staff at the center, and the development and implementation of a support plan for the child.

Such processes can ensure the continued growth and development of the children and the improvement of the service's behavioral guidance policies.

5.17 Policy on Compliance with Child Abuse and Neglect Reporting Laws

The child care service should require all employees and care providers of child care services, including consultants and trainers, to report all suspected cases of child abuse or neglect to designated local authorities.

The report may be done directly by the teacher/care provider or the family child care provider or through the program manager or director.

Child care personnel often are in the best position to recognize the signs of possible child abuse or neglect. Teaching responsibility for reporting child abuse or neglect as well as the state and local laws about reporting should be an essential part of the orientation program of the child care service. Personnel should be aware that violations of state or local child abuse and neglect reporting laws may invoke civil or criminal penalties, and/or civil suits for damages.

5.18 Policy on Confidentiality of Information in Child Abuse and Neglect Cases

At all times, the child care service should maintain the child's and family's right to privacy, as required by state and federal law. During the course of a child abuse investigation, the child care service should work cooperatively with the staff of the investigating agency.

Violations of confidentiality statutes should be dealt with by appropriate civil and criminal penalties.

State and federal laws should contain clear guidelines governing the practice of confidentiality and the permissible sharing of information regarding cases of child abuse or neglect. These laws should be written to facilitate interagency cooperation, coordination, and communication; to protect children; and to promote the provision of early intervention services to families, as needed.

When child protection involves cross-jurisdictional communication (e.g., the military, tribal councils, interstate or international moves), written agreements and protocols should be established that permit the sharing of appropriate information falling within these confidentiality guidelines. Where state laws prohibit sharing information across jurisdictional boundaries, thus inhibiting the protection of children, the child care service should advocate for statutory changes.

5.19 The Role of Parents in the Governance of the Child Care Service and Its Programs

The child care service should involve parents in determining the programs and policies of the child care service and its sponsoring agency.

Parents should be included on the governing board of the voluntary agency and on the child care advisory committee.

The special skills and talents that parents can offer include the following:

- As aides, parents may make home visits under staff supervision, encourage other parents to take part in the program, serve as channels of communication between the parents and staff, and help other parents make good use of available community resources.

- Parents may be useful in the recruitment of family child care homes and group child care homes.

- Parents can be effective partners in advocacy efforts to increase needed child care and other community resources and to promote the services necessary to strengthen and preserve families with children.

- Parents can help to ensure that culturally competent and high-quality services are provided.

Accountability

5.20 Maintenance of Standards

The child care service should continually evaluate its functions, policies, and practices on the basis of the Child Welfare League of America Standards of Excellence, and in accordance with the standards established by accrediting organizations.

5.21 Regulatory Requirements

The state or tribal jurisdiction and the local jurisdiction should license and regulate all forms of child care regardless of the auspices under which they are provided. All child care providers should meet state or tribal and local licensing requirements, and all other regulations designed to protect the health and safety of children.

The National Association for the Education of Young Children states in its position statement (NAEYC, 2002), that quality child care can be achieved only if the standards regulating it:

(1) require developmentally appropriate curricula,

(2) include strong supports for children and their families,

(3) are enacted in ways appropriate for young children, and

(4) are developed through comprehensive processes.

State and tribal or local jurisdictions should work to improve the objectivity of the regulations and work toward the standardization of licensing and regulation. Enforcement techniques should be strong and decisive, and enforced consistently. They may include fines and penalties.

Many jurisdictions have turned toward tiered licensing systems (see Introduction, p. 28) as a means of regulating the child care system and rewarding the best programs and facilities.

The community assumes a social and legal responsibility for the care and protection of its children when it sanctions the operation of child care providers. Licensing and other regulatory requirements help to assure that providers will offer a minimum standard of care and protection for children outside of their homes. Responsibility for the care and protection of children must be shared by parents, governmental licensing authorities, and child care providers by adhering strictly to legal regulations.

The goal of state child care licensing is to protect the health, safety, and well-being of children in child care settings. Child care licensing requirements provide basic protections by the state for children in these settings by reflecting the state's minimum health and safety standards. Effective child care licensing requires:

- review and revision of the regulations on a regular basis to incorporate new knowledge and understanding of the field;

- regular technical assistance and consultation to improve the quality of care delivered to children;

- monitoring of providers, including random, unannounced visits on a yearly basis;

- enforcement through efforts that include incentives, fines, and penalties;

- protected caseloads for child care licensing staff, ensuring that the licensor is able to perform his or her functions well and to have sufficient interaction with the child care staff and/or provider;

- well-prepared licensors with a minimum of a four-year college degree in a related field and a background in child development through education or experience in the child care field;

- tools for assessing and monitoring the child care setting;

- access by licensors to ongoing professional development and annual inservice training; and

- opportunities for licensors to collaborate with other agencies to enhance community services.

Ensuring Quality

5.22 Continuous Quality Improvement

The child care service should develop and conduct a continuous quality improvement program that is integrated throughout all aspects of the program to ensure a culture of continuous improvement in the quality of its services.

The agency should evaluate its programs and services regularly to ensure that services are delivered according to best practice standards and that interventions and treatment methods used are evidence based.

5.23 Components of the Continuous Quality Improvement Program (CQI)

The child care service should provide procedures for monitoring agency performance and for measuring and enhancing program effectiveness.

The child care service quality improvement program may include, as appropriate to the size and type of child care service:

- systematic data collection and analysis directed to key indicators, goals for improvement, and problem identification and solving;
- objective measures of performance (using standardized or recognized tools when possible) such as indicators of client safety and developmental progress;
- periodic, regular review of case records;
- measures of satisfaction from relevant stakeholders and clients;
- a reporting system that includes management, board of directors, staff, and stakeholders, and identifies current trends, strengths, concerns, and opportunities for improvement;
- data collection on incidences of injury or illness including age of child and circumstance;
- review systems designed to monitor the developmental progress of the children and the degree of parental involvement and satisfaction;

- a peer review component for staff qualifications, standards of care, and critical incident review;
- involvement by staff at every level of the organization in planning, benchmarking, and problem identification and resolution;
- coordination with the agency's external accreditation program, if applicable, to prevent duplication of effort;
- review of program designs and outcomes to ensure that services are operating as intended and are producing desired results in the most efficient manner;
- literature review and updating to current research in the field to promote best practice and interventions that are proven to be effective; and
- a review and redesign mechanism, whereby the quality system itself is periodically reviewed for its effectiveness and corrective action is taken as needed.

5.24 Evaluating Program Performance and Achievement of Child, Family, and Service Goals

To improve the quality of the services provided, the child care service should regularly evaluate the effectiveness of its services in terms of quality assurance and client satisfaction to improve the quality of the services provided.

Depending on the program's size and type, the evaluation may be conducted by qualified agency staff or outside consultants.

For larger, multiservice programs, it should be developed and implemented using a team approach, including agency program and evaluation staff.

Although most evaluations will be planned, the agency should have the ability to formally evaluate critical incidents and respond to ad hoc requests. The evaluation should be used to assess program performance in meeting the goals and outcomes of the program.

The agency should assess the implications of the evaluation findings for:

- service delivery, individual practice, program operations, and its staff; and

- the allocation process, particularly if the findings indicate a need to reassign staff or financial resources.

Program and practice modifications should occur when indicated by the evaluation findings.

5.25 Integration of Quality Improvement and Program Evaluation Findings

A quality improvement committee should regularly monitor the child care service's quality improvement and program evaluation procedures, systematically analyze quality improvement and program evaluation information, and make recommendations to the agency's decisionmakers regarding needed changes or improvements.

The child care service's quality improvement program should be integrated through such activities as:

- quarterly reports consisting of trends in demographics and service utilization;
- a training curriculum covering staff responsibilities pertinent to the substantive functions of the agency; and
- documentation describing the quality improvement program, with instructions to staff members regarding their responsibilities for completing CQI forms and tasks.

5.26 Risk Management Program

The agency should have in place policies and procedures to prevent or respond to agency and staff liability in providing residential services. The agency providing a child care service should carry liability insurance and have a risk management program to reduce liability that includes training in risk identification and instruction on how to minimize risk.

Risk management procedures should take into account surrounding environmental risk factors in addition to the standard evaluations considered for risk management.

The risk management policies of the child care service should be in accord with CWLA's *Standards of Excellence for the Management and Governance of Child Welfare Agencies* (1996) and the standards of the Council on Accreditation (COA) and NAEYC (1998).

5.27 Advocacy

To promote the best interests of the children and families served, the child care service, working with parents and other community organizations, should maintain a strong advocacy effort.

Parents and those involved in providing the child care service should take responsibility for enhancing the child care resources in their community, with a strategic discussion of how to get the most impact from the advocacy effort, including what the service's role should be in the community.

The advocacy effort should be used:

- to build a constituency of community members concerned with children's issues;
- to stimulate awareness of and involvement in activities to improve the quality of care in the community;
- as an opportunity to highlight the public's investment in children;
- to obtain adequate funding;
- as an ongoing activity of the child care service;
- to propose, support, or oppose local, state, and federal advocacy efforts related to improvements in the child care systems;
- to influence the state's biennial planning process for the federal child care and development block grant program; and
- as a marketing and public relations function of the child care service.

6

Support Systems

Three components are essential to a comprehensive child care system: child care resource and referral services, family child care/network systems, and child care subsidy systems. The goals for each of these components, as well as standards specific to each, are presented here.

CHILD CARE RESOURCE AND REFERRAL

Goals

I. The child care resource and referral service works to develop quality child care in the community.

II. In carrying out its mission, the child care resource and referral provides services to multiple clients, including parents and their children, providers, and the community at large.

III. The child care resource and referral service accomplishes its mission through the following core services: parent counseling for child care and family services, professional development of the child care workforce, tracking supply and demand, stimulating increase in supply, and advocacy for quality and community education.

6.1   Definition of Child Care Resource and Referral

The child care resource and referral service is a community-based service that works for the development of quality child care.

The resource and referral service should:

- offer parents consultation and assistance in the search for quality child care;
- offer children enhanced resources for safe and developmentally appropriate care;
- be responsive to emerging issues;
- offer providers consultation, including technical assistance, training, and support;
- offer the community data, planning, policy analysis, education, and advocacy on child care needs and supply.
- educate parents and empower them to make choices;
- provide family support services (e.g., mental health, parent training);
- work to expand child care resources in the community;
- develop community linkages with private and public agencies related to children and family services; and
- provide training and/or technical assistance to providers.

6.2   Clients Served by the Child Care Resource and Referral Service

The child care resource and referral service should serve multiple clients, including parents and their children, providers, and the community.

The guiding principle of the resource and referral service should be the well-being of children and their families, and the development of quality child care for them. The resource and referral service should:

- assist parents in their efforts to obtain quality child care;
- support providers' efforts to deliver quality child care; and
- work with the community to improve access to, and the availability of, affordable child care for children and families.

Every resource and referral service should have a written policy available to the community for reference about how the service handles referrals.

No resource and referral service should provide referrals to any agency or individual operating an illegal child care program.

Some forms of child care are legally exempt from state child care licensing because they fall under different rules (e.g., afterschool programs operated on school property, or family child care homes with certain numbers of children). The resource and referral service should encourage and support the regulation of all forms of child care.

Resource and Referral Core Services

The resource and referral service should offer to parents, child care providers, and the community a group of core services integral to the conduct of its responsibilities.

These core responsibilities provide a strong, basic outline of what all resource and referral services should strive for:

- parent counseling about child care and family resources,
- development of the child care profession through training and outreach,
- documentation and analysis of child care supply and demand,
- advocacy to improve the quality of child care,
- community education about child care concerns and parents' needs, and
- increasing the supply of child care in communities.

6.3   Core Services to Parents and Their Children

The resource and referral service should help parents become educated consumers of quality child care.

The resource and referral service should operate from the philosophic position that parents can and will make the best choices for their children given an adequate supply of affordable, accessible quality child care and the information necessary to make the proper choice.

The assistance offered by the resource and referral service to parents searching for child care should be given in a manner that promotes parental choice, recognizes their responsibility in selecting appropriate child care for their children, makes referrals and not recommendations, and maximizes parental access to child care resources.

To these ends, the resource and referral service should provide the following services to parents and their children:

- counsel parents on how best to meet their specific child care needs by furnishing information on selecting quality care and by making referrals to services that are accessible and affordable to them;
- provide information to parents about the range of available, legally operating child care providers so they can expand their options;
- connect parents with other agencies and services that will support them in caring for their young children;
- empower parents to become advocates for their own children by educating them about what to ask of their child care provider, and what to look for in monitoring the care provided;
- provide impartial referrals to parents that show respect for their rights of confidentiality, are sensitive to their dignity, culture, values, and beliefs, and, when possible, are presented in the language commonly used by the family;
- be housed in a convenient, accessible location for the community it serves;
- be familiar with the laws that protect children served by child care providers and provide that information to parents;
- educate parents about child care policies on the local, state, and national levels; and
- assist parents in finding out if they are eligible for financial assistance.

6.4 Core Services to Providers

The resource and referral service should support existing provider systems in the community and facilitate the development and expansion of the quality care that is responsive to local needs and conditions.

The services offered to providers should include:

- providing technical assistance to new and existing providers to assist in the delivery of quality services;
- providing parent referrals to all types of legally operating child care providers within its service areas;
- maintaining a current list of all legally operating providers with referrals made without charge to providers regardless of the provider's status as a nonprofit or for-profit organization;
- providing technical assistance to existing and potential child care providers on start-up and operating procedures, as well as on regulations, including, but not limited to, licensing, zoning, program, and budget development, and assistance in obtaining pertinent information on these subjects from other sources;
- collecting and reporting communitywide statistics on the need and availability of child care;
- facilitating communication among child care providers and other community child-related services;
- ensuring that all community providers have knowledge about training opportunities to further professional staff development through collaboration with available community agencies;
- disseminating information on current trends and public issues affecting the local, state, or national delivery of child care;
- publishing the resource and referral referral and complaint polices and procedures;
- helping with data collection of providers' information to be used for recruitment and retention of staff;
- respecting provider confidentiality and privacy; and

- supporting providers around their professional development, especially compensation and benefits.

6.5   Core Services to the Community

The resource and referral service should make the community and its leaders aware of child care issues and the need for available and affordable quality services.

To build this awareness, resource and referral services should provide the following supports to the communities they serve:

- develop and disseminate current information on selecting quality child care and on children's activities, parent education, and provider training;
- collect needs assessment and supply and demand data;
- disseminate and share data with community leaders about child care and engage them in addressing identified needs;
- help government agencies, employers, private businesses, and social service agencies increase their knowledge of child care issues, and encourage them to respond to parent and provider needs;
- ensure visibility of the service by advertising efforts (e.g., listing in the local yellow pages);
- work with the community's child- and family-service agencies to enhance their aid to young children and their families; and
- educate private citizens about community child care needs in its publications and public information efforts.

Optional Resource and Referral Services

A range of optional services may complement the core resource and referral services as a response to the expressed needs of parents, providers, and the community.

6.6 Criteria for Initiating an Optional Service

The resource and referral service should consider optional services if they would be responsive to emerging issues; improve the service's ability to supply technical assistance to child care providers; improve the service's ability to collect and regularly update data on child care; improve the service's ability to educate the parents, providers, or the community; improve the effectiveness of the delivery of information to parents concerning child care; expand the availability of child care, improve its quality, or make it more accessible; and not duplicate any existing, accessible service, but address identified gaps in services and work toward filling them.

6.7 Optional Services

The resource and referral agency should consider the following optional services: exploring financial assistance options, organizing providers into self-support networks to be advocacy groups in their own behalf, providing mental health services, conducting market rate surveys, administering a public subsidy system, creating family support/parenting services (e.g., parenting education), creating early literacy projects (e.g., helping parents read to the children), and creating a centralized eligibility list.

6.8 Administering the Resource and Referral Service

The resource and referral service, as an entity responsible for delivering services to the public, should conform to the administrative policies and procedures described in Chapter 5 of this volume.

6.9 Representing the Community

The resource and referral service should serve as the community representative for child care resource and referral services.

The resource and referral service should collaborate with providers and other community organizations to define appropriate roles and relationships, including the role of the resource and referral service in representing the community.

The resource and referral service should be a member of local child care planning councils and other planning bodies and be involved in early childhood initiatives.

6.10 Delivering Fair and Equitable Services

The child care resource and referral service should assure the fair and equitable delivery of all its services.

The resource and referral service should have written referral policies that note the criteria for providers being included on the referral files, the process for completing an application, and the process for providing a copy of a current and valid license.

The resource and referral service should affirm parental choice in child care decisions.

The resource and referral service should promote parental choice by providing parents with the entire range of child care options available to them and with guidance in making an appropriate choice for themselves and their children.

The resource and referral service should not recommend any particular type of care or any individual providers.

The resource and referral service should make referrals, not recommendations. Listing with the resource and referral is not a guarantee that parents will select child care providers.

The resource and referral service should not discriminate against individuals or groups, whether parents or providers, on the basis of gender, race or ethnicity, national origin or ancestry, religion, age, disability, or sexual orientation.

6.11 Providing Comprehensive Services

The resource and referral service should be a comprehensive service for its designated geographic area by providing all of the core services (see 6.3–6.5).

6.12 Serving All Types of Families

The resource and referral organization should serve all types of families, regardless of income level; cultural, religious, or ethnic background; or physical, mental, or emotional disability.

6.13 Community-Based Services

The resource and referral service should be community based and conveniently located to a substantial number of its clients. It should have a local identity and a strong involvement in community decisionmaking.

6.14 Confidentiality

The resource and referral service should treat as confidential any and all information about the children and families it serves, only sharing the information with child care service providers on a need-to-know basis.

6.15 Restrictive Services

To avoid coming into conflict with its own purposes, the resource and referral service should restrict itself from participating in certain child care activities (see 6.20).

The resource and referral service should avoid:

• acting as a regulator of child care, and
• controlling or helping to determine the recipients of contracts or funds allocated to child care providers.

6.16 Funding Base

The resource and referral service should develop short and long term plans for services based upon resources available.

6.17 Sound Business Practices

The resource and referral service should follow sound business practices, personnel policies, and operating procedures.

6.18 Staffing

The resource and referral service should develop a professional staff that is experienced in working with parents, knowledgeable about quality child care practices, and able to develop working relationships with providers of all forms of care.

6.19 Liability

The resource and referral service should maintain adequate liability insurance, while using referral procedures that limit the risk of liability.

6.20 Conflict of Interest

The resource and referral service should have a conflict-of-interest policy that facilitates its role as an impartial referral source. It should assure the fair and equitable delivery of all its services.

In some circumstances, agencies that operate resource and referral services should be permitted to operate their own direct services as long as they have a clear conflict-of-interest policy. Often agencies with resource and referral services are asked to open specific child care facilities to fill an unmet need within a community. Resource and referral services are in the unique position of identifying these gaps in service and assisting in the development of a service response, either directly or in collaboration with other providers and community agencies.

Providing the direct service is allowable only if the referral service and the direct service do not share staff, resource and referral staff continue to make referrals based on the best interests of the children and families, and there is open communication between the agency operating the resource and referral and other direct service providers to ensure that there is no perceived conflict of interest (see 6.15).

6.21 Conducting a Needs Analysis and Advocating to Address Unmet Needs

The resource and referral agency should continuously document and analyze the actual supply of and demand for child care services in the community, to identify gaps and advocate for their reduction.

The documentation of need and existing supply should help the child care market operate more efficiently and produce a broad picture of the market.

6.22 Conducting Child Care Policy Analyses

The resource and referral service should collect data from child care providers and use this information to analyze child care policies on the local, state, and national levels.

6.23 Maintaining Data on Requests for Services

The resource and referral service should maintain ongoing documentation of requests for services during the referral process.

These records should be made at the time of referral and should include, but not be limited to:

- number of calls,
- ages of children,
- type of care requested,
- time category of child care requested for each child,
- special time category needed,
- reason child care is needed, and
- geographical area.

The information should be maintained in such a manner that it is easily accessible for dissemination.

6.24 Maintaining Data on Providers

The resource and referral service should maintain records on all providers in the community.

The provider information should include, but not be limited to:

- location,
- phone number,
- type of program,
- hours of service,

- age of children served,
- fees and eligibility for services,
- specific program information, and
- specific information on services for children with disabilities.

Information on providers, including whether they have any openings, should be updated on a quarterly basis.

6.25 Promulgating Data on Rates and Availability

The resource and referral service should supply for parents, providers, and the community accurate information, data collection, and documentation about the rates for child care, openings, waiting lists, and centralized eligibility lists.

6.26 Evaluating the Resource and Referral Service

The resource and referral service should develop and use a set of written criteria to measure the effectiveness of its work.

The criteria should include collecting follow-up data with families to determine if the referral information was helpful.

FAMILY CHILD CARE NETWORKS/SYSTEMS

Goals

I. The family child care network/system, whether stand-alone or part of a larger agency, has a clearly defined structure and provides both direct and indirect services to family child care providers.

II. The family child care network/system strengthens the capacity of independent family child care providers by helping the provider with quality improvement, curriculum development, and administrative tasks including subsidies, accreditation, and marketing.

III. The family child care network/system provides a wide range of services to children in care and their families.

Family child care providers can partner with other independent family child care providers or with previously formed networks/systems to provide some of the services and accomplish some of the goals that child care centers are able to accomplish because they work on a larger scale. These networks or systems vary depending on the needs of the providers and families they serve, but they should all share some basic structure and goals.

6.27 Structure

Family child care networks may be part of a larger agency or a stand-alone agency. The family child care network should have a clearly defined structure with key parts.

Leadership of the service should be in the hands of a board of directors and/or executive director, who will determine the direction of the agency, make any bids for funds or subsidies, lead advocacy efforts, oversee training of direct providers and staff, and supervise network/system staff.

Family child care network/system staff should include individuals responsible for financial management, direct services (e.g., home visitors, parent support, specialized direct services), and administrative supports.

Administrative Services

Family child care networks should support the indirect services provided by family child care providers.

The network/system does not detract from the independent nature of the family child care providers, but instead works in association with the provider to help with subsidies, accreditation, and marketing.

6.28 Accessing and Managing Funds

The family child care network should apply for and manage any local, state, federal, or full pay subsidies provided to children in the network served by family child care homes.

6.29 Outreach and Recruitment of Providers

The family child care network should ensure that new family child care and group child care homes are recruited by interpreting the program to the community. Special methods such as publicity campaigns, direct appeals to selected groups, and an individualized approach to particular families by agency staff members, including current family child care and group child care providers, and parents should be used.

Caring for children during the day should recognized as having the status of employment and should be viewed as an important contribution to the community.

The family child care network should work with providers during start up to provide consultation and training in both business development and early childhood development-related fields.

The family child care network should offer consultation and advice on licensing procedures prior to the opening of the home-based business.

6.30 Screening and Selection of Family Child Care and Group Child Care Providers

The family child care network should ensure that providers who apply to care for a child or children during the day in their own homes are screened to determine whether they are suitable to provide the required care.

The screening process should include:

- interviews with the prospective family child care or group child care provider and other members of the family, including the children, in a language they all understand;
- visits to the home; and
- professional as well as personal references from nonrelatives.

The screening process should clarify how the family child care network and the provider can best work together with regard to:

- responsibilities of the provider,

- required hours of care,
- responsibilities of the child care service staff,
- daily activities for the children,
- rate of payment and responsibility for payment,
- opportunities for training and staff development, and
- state and local regulatory requirements and procedures.

The staff member conducting the interview should discuss with the applicant how best to approach problems that arise regarding:

- the child's experience of separation twice a day, and
- the provider's sharing the caregiving of the child with child's own parents.

The staff members responsible for recruitment should evaluate prospective family child care and group child care providers and the ways in which they are likely to perform, indicating:

- whether the applicant has the potential for meeting the needs of the children and parents served by the child care service;
- whether the applicant can deliver culturally competent services;
- whether the applicant can respect and support parents as the primary caregivers of their child;
- whether the applicant can identify the program and goals of the child care service, work within its policies, share responsibilities appropriately, and work with the designated staff member;
- the type and number of children whom the home can best serve; and
- the kinds of continuing support that would be beneficial.

The staff member's evaluation of the prospective family child care and group child care provider should be presented and recorded. This will enable other members of the family child care network staff to make optimum use of the provider as a resource for children who may benefit from a family child care or group child care home experience.

6.31 Orientation of New Providers

The family child care network should make sure that new providers entering into the network understand the relationship between them and the responsibilities of each.

This can be accomplished through a series of steps.

(1) Before contracting with the provider, the network should explain the relationship and ensure that the provider has had basic training and/or knowledge in the field of family child care.

(2) The network should conduct a site visit to check the condition of the home and assess the provider's motives for starting a service.

(3) The network should explain the basic business principles of running a family child care home to the provider so he or she is aware of aspects of the decision to provide care.

These steps should be thoroughly explored before a contract is signed so that both sides understand the commitment being made.

6.32 Contracting

The family child care network should ensure that the provider/network contract makes clear the relationship between the network/system and the provider.

The nature of this relationship, whether an employer/employee or contractual in nature, should be clearly stated in the contract. Any limitations or responsibilities should be explicitly laid out.

The method of provider payment should be described in the contract as well as parent fee collection methods and procedures. These will vary based on the nature of the relationship and thus must be clearly understood by both the provider and the network.

Finally, the contract should explain any and all support services that the system will offer to the providers.

6.33 Recordkeeping

The family child care network should ensure that both the provider and the network have copies of the current license; documentation of home visits; first aid and CPR certification; health and safety checklist; signed system/home network contract (renewed annually); dates, content, and duration of orientation training; documentation of all system-provided training attended by the provider and related certificates; awards and credentials; any complaints/incidents concerning the provider by a parent or another source; verification of participation in the child and adult care food program, where applicable; and site specific information for each home provider describing play area, pets, etc., for referral purposes.

Services to Children and Families

In addition to serving the providers contracted with the network (see 6.31, 6.44–6.46), family child care network/ systems should also serve directly the families and children in the care of their providers.

6.34 Referrals

The family child care network/system should refer parents to providers in a manner that ensures parental choice and does not discriminate against any child or parent based on religion, age, race, ethnicity, income, or disability.

6.35 Intake

When determining eligibility for subsidized care, the family child care network should hold meetings with the parents/ guardians as part of the enrollment process.

In these meetings information should be gathered and the system and its policies should be explained and agreed on by both the parent/guardian and the provider.

6.36 Recordkeeping

The family child care network/system should maintain a file on each family receiving subsidized care.

This record should include

- documentation of the attempts made to meet the child/children's needs;
- documentation of efforts to enhance development;
- documentation required for compliance with subsidy systems;
- copies of written correspondence with the family;
- documentation of a developmental profile or assessment; and
- documentation of the child's progress, taken every six months.

6.37 Communication

The family child care network/system should promote provider/parent communication and should provide mediation when necessary.

6.38 Parental Involvement

The family child care network/system should provide opportunities for parents to participate in the development and evaluation of their child/children's programs. The network should conduct an annual parent survey to measure their satisfaction with the services being provided to them and their children.

6.39 Networking

The family child care network/system should work with local community organizations and provide referrals when necessary.

6.40 Child Assessment and Observation

The family child care network/system should conduct regular observation and assessment of the children in their providers' care at least every six months during their regular home visits.

6.41 Policy on Compliance with Child Abuse and Neglect Reporting Laws

The family child care network/system should require all employees and independent family child care providers, including consultants and trainers, to report all suspected cases of child abuse or neglect to designated local authorities. The report may be done directly by the family child care provider or through the program manager or director.

Child care personnel and family child care providers often are in the best position to recognize the signs of possible child abuse or neglect. Teaching responsibility for reporting child abuse or neglect as well as the state and local laws about reporting should be an essential part of the orientation program of the child care service. Personnel and family child care providers should be aware that violations of state or local child abuse and neglect reporting laws might invoke civil or criminal penalties, and/or civil suits for damages.

At all times, the family child care network/system should maintain the child's and family's right to privacy, as required by state and federal law. During the course of a child abuse investigation, the family child care network/system should work cooperatively with the staff of the investigating agency. Violations of confidentiality statutes should be dealt with according to appropriate civil and criminal statutes (see 5.15).

6.42 Continuity of Care

The family child care network/system staff should monitor backup care arrangements, support enrollment of children in care through subsidy, and support parent/provider communication.

The family child care network/system staff should play a role in the transition of a child out of the family child care home to another arrangement when it is time for the child to move on.

6.43 Transportation

If the family child care network/system provides transportation of any kind, the network should ensure adherence to the regulations and policies of the state Department of Motor Vehicles and all other related state agencies and should ensure appropriate liability insurance.

Services to Providers

All family child care networks/systems should strive to provide a wide range of services to their contracted providers, developing trust and communication between the provider and the network/system.

6.44 Provider Visits

The family child care network/system should conduct monthly visits to each of its providers to ensure quality care.

At least four of these visits each year should be unannounced visits.

6.45 Marketing

The family child care network/system should serve as a system of referrals for the provider.

The network should have a clearly stated policy for referrals. In addition, the network may advertise providers in key locations.

6.46 Training and Professional Development

The family child care network/system should offer a minimum of 20 hours training annually on a variety of early childhood development/care and business topics.

This training should cover a wide range of topics but focus on emerging research and findings in the early childhood education field and topics affecting small business owners

In addition, each system should work with providers on an annual professional development plan that includes the goals of the provider and the network for the year, plans for site improvement, educational attainment, etc. The system should help providers attain these goals and work with them to attain recognized credentials (e.g., National Association

for Family Child Care accreditation, Child Development Associate certification).

Networking

The family child care network/system should compile information on community resources and make this available
to providers. In addition, the network should offer help in
making referrals of children to outside services.

6.47 Communication

The family child care network/system should promote positive
parent/provider communications and act as a mediator when
necessary.

6.48 Food Program Enrollment

The family child care network/system should make available
information on local USDA-sponsored food programs (e.g., Child
and Adult Care Food Program) to providers, require participation where possible, and assist with enrollment.

6.49 Emergency Support

The family child care network/system staff should be available
to providers at all hours that the home is providing child care.

> The family child care network/system staff should have
> beepers or cell phones to ensure their accessibility

6.50 Backup Care Arrangements

The family child care network/system should help providers
arrange for substitute care should the provider need time off.

> Choice should be given to parents regarding where their
> child will be should backup care be necessary. Such arrange-
> ments should be made well in advance.

> The substitute provider should receive all relevant reports
> and information about the children for whom they will be
> providing care.

6.51 Special Events

When possible, the family child care network/system should offer opportunities for providers to meet, share information with, and provide social support to other providers (e.g., field trips, appreciation events).

6.52 Equipment Lending/Loan Program

The family child care network/system should offer support and assistance to providers through loans or through equipment lending.

> Equipment that providers could not otherwise afford can be loaned to providers or sold at reduced rates by the network/system.

> In addition, the network/system can offer direct loans to enable providers to purchase equipment of their own.

Staffing the Network/System

> The staff of the family child care network/system should have clearly defined roles in serving providers, children, and families and should meet certain levels of education and training to ensure the quality of the services provided.

6.53 Staff Providing Services to Providers

The family child care network staff who provide direct services to providers (e.g., professional development, curriculum development, referrals, etc.) should have at least a bachelor's degree in early childhood education or a related field.

> For those providing specialized services to child care providers, a master's degree in their field of work is recommended.

> Once hired, staff should continue training and education in the field of early childhood education.

6.54 Staff Providing Services to Parents and Families

The family child care network staff who provide direct services to parents of children in the child care network/system (e.g., access to substitute care, referrals, etc.), should have at a minimum a high school diploma with two years of experience in child care or a related field. In addition, staff should have training in the form of completed college courses or an associate's degree in early childhood education or a related field.

Staff transporting children should have a proper state driver's license.

6.55 Staff Providing Services to Children

The family child care network staff who provide direct services to children enrolled in the network/system (e.g., observation of children, referrals to therapeutic services) should have a high school diploma and at least two years experience in child care or a related field. A specialized degree in health services, mental health services, social work, behavior management, or any other specialized service they may be providing to children in the network/system is desirable. In addition, they should be given appropriate on-the-job-training.

Once hired, staff should continue to receive training and take classes in the early childhood development field.

CHILD CARE SUBSIDY SYSTEMS
Goals

   I. Eligible families receive an subsidy adequate to meet their child care needs.

   II. Parents have the necessary resources to purchase child care.

   III. Families receiving subsidies are able to choose the type of care they prefer for their children.

6.56 Development of a State Child Care Subsidy System

Each state should develop a child care subsidy system designed to provide publicly funded child care subsidies to families determined to be eligible to receive such subsidies.

Some systems are operated by the state in local and regional state offices. In other states, the management of the child care subsidy system is contracted out to a group of either for-profit companies and/or nonprofit agencies, while in others, the functions of the child care subsidy system are split between public and private agencies.

The federally funded child care subsidy system expanded greatly in the 1990s with the passage of the Child Care and Development Block Grant (CCDBG) and then with the changes in the country's welfare laws (see Introduction, p. 6). With the goal of getting parents on welfare into the workforce, additional child care funds were made available to states through CCDBG. A portion of the funding is also used to provide subsidies to low-income working families to help them pay for the child care expenses.

6.57 Enrollment of Children in the Subsidy Program

The agency should not discriminate on the basis of sex, sexual orientation, gender, ethnic group identification, race, ancestry, national origin, religion, color, or mental or physical disability in determining which children are served. Additionally, the agency should welcome enrollment of children with disabilities, understand the requirements of the Americans with Disabilities Act to make reasonable accommodations to such children, and then clearly implement those accommodations.

6.58 Outreach and Public Awareness

Child care subsidy systems should make every effort possible to let all families know that child care subsidies are available for eligible families, the criteria for eligibility, and how and where to apply for a subsidy.

All outreach and public awareness information should be available in multiple languages reflecting the linguistic diversity of the community. Outreach efforts should include newsletters, fliers, news releases, speaking engagements, and community service activities.

6.59 Parental Choice

The policies of the child care subsidy system should be developed to ensure that parents have the ability to choose the type of care they prefer.

Parents should be referred to the local child care resource and referral agency or other designated agency to assist them in making an appropriate choice of care provider for their child (see 6.3). They should receive information about the impact that quality child care has on the developmental needs of their child and how to look for better quality care.

State and local payment policies should promote sound parental decisionmaking and should not adversely affect parental choices. Parent fees should be based on the family's income and family size rather than on the type of care chosen. Higher parent fees should not be instituted for higher quality care, center-based care, or for programs that meet higher accreditation standards. Parents should continue to pay the sliding scale rate regardless of the type of care provided.

All programs and providers participating in the child care subsidy system should be required to meet health and safety standards to ensure that children are in healthy and safe child care settings.

Families should be able to select from 3 types of child care:

- *Licensed center-based care:* Center-based care (child care centers) offers child care, development, and education services to children on a part-time or full-time basis. Child care centers can be designed for different age groups (infants, toddler, preschool, and school age) of children. The centers are regulated by a state or local government entity and must follow licensing requirements. These requirements are designed to promote health, safety, and encourage a better child care setting for children.

- *Family child care and group child care homes:* A family child care or group child care home is licensed or registered and regulated through a state or local government entity. Family child care and group child care homes offer a homelike setting. Family child care and group homes have fewer children in care than centers. This allows the provider to offer the children individual attention. Family child care and group child care homes may have more flexible hours for families and some providers may be open nights and weekends.

• *Licensed-exempt care:* Relatives or nonrelatives may provide care that is exempt from a state or local government's licensing regulations.

Each state's licensing law defines the care that must be regulated. Some states exempt child care settings operated by a government or faith-based agency. Some states exempt care in a family child care home that is provided for a small number of children. Most states exempt care provided by relatives.

All exempt providers should clear a required fingerprint and background investigation. This should be a service to all families seeking a child care provider. This service should be able to check for criminal and child abuse convictions. Providers' fingerprints should be checked against a criminal history system, a child abuse central listing, and FBI records. In addition, a health and safety certification should be developed and implemented to ensure the best environment for the children.

6.60 Parental Access

Parents should have unlimited access to their children and the providers caring for their children during normal hours of provider operation and whenever their children are in the care of the provider.

This policy should be included in parent handbooks, contracts, and other parent-support materials, as well as in all provider agreements.

6.61 Family Eligibility

Child care subsidy systems should be designed to serve the entire family and not individual children within the family.

Child care subsidies should be available to families moving off of welfare due to employment as well as to low-income working families.

For most families, eligibility requirements should be based on income guidelines and the service needs of the parents and the child. Child care subsidies should be available to families with income up to 85% of each state's median income. This amount should be adjusted annually to reflect changes in each state's state median income calculation. The income guideline should be waived for families in the protective service system and for children in foster care.

Child care subsidies should be available to income-eligible families to allow parents to work, to seek and attend educational institutions, or to participate in work-training opportunities. Determination of eligibility should be done in manner that does not create obstacles for families.

Families should have a reasonable amount of time, not to exceed 30 days, to gather and submit all required documentation. The state subsidy system should allow for convenient locations and ample hours to serve working families, along with face-to-face meetings with case managers to establish strong working relationships with each program. The agency should verify the eligibility and need of each family or child within 30 days of a change in status or at intervals not to exceed 12 months. Redetermination should be allowed in ways that do not require in-person appointments.

State systems should be required to maintain an eligibility list of all families who have applied.

- Systems should not discourage families from applying due to an existing long eligibility list.
- The eligibility list should be kept current and should be accessible online.
- The subsidy system should inform parents in writing when it is time to update the list before deleting names. Families should be able to remain on the eligibility list as long as they have a need for care. Eligibility lists should be updated in six-month intervals to ensure the family data remains accurate.

6.62   Providing Supportive Case Management Services

The child care subsidy system should provide supportive case management services to the families and providers involved in the program.

Case management should be provided through either a comprehensive services model or specialized support services model.

- In the comprehensive services model, case managers serve families and providers in all aspects of their interaction with the agency.
- In the specialized support services model, case management is broken down into specific elements of the process, such as intake, payment, or eligibility.

In either case, a best practice approach should be implemented, with a focus on providing seamless support to the families and providers. The services should be easily understood and uninterrupted by the case management process. All steps involved in accessing the program should be made available to families through a parent handbook.

The agency should establish an appeal process for families. Any notice of action or other adverse decision made by the agency should be eligible for the appeal process. Such a process should include a 14-day prior notice of any adverse action, along with specific guidelines for processing the appeal. The appeal policy and procedures should emphasize the rights of families within the program.

6.63 Provider Reimbursement Rates

The public agency should develop policies and regulations that support provider participation, create incentives for participation, and do not establish obstacles that would reduce participation.

The subsidy system should create maximum reimbursement rate ceilings at 100% of the local and regional market rate. The rate ceiling should be increased annually to reflect a cost of living adjustment and biennially to reflect increases in the market rate. Market rate surveys should be conducted biennially.

State systems should institute tiered-reimbursement provider rates to reflect the higher cost of providing higher quality care. The tiered reimbursement rate system will be an incentive for programs to offer higher quality services.

Parents should not be required to pay higher parent fees based on a tiered-reimbursement rate system (see 6.59).

Child care programs and providers should receive payment for the state subsidy directly from the child care subsidy system. The payment should be made in a timely manner with responsive case management available to help quickly and accurately resolve any discrepancies. Parent fees should be paid directly to the provider or the program. Parents should not have to pay a fee in addition to the one established by the subsidy system. Subsidy systems should pay for a reasonable amount of absent days and should design a system that does not penalize a program or a provider for children who may not need full time care.

6.64 Provider Technical Assistance

The child care subsidy system should offer technical assistance to all providers to guarantee the success of their participation.

Agencies administering child care subsidies should meet with providers and perform site visits to help to maintain and foster a harmonious communication.

Agencies should offer workshops and classes to providers to help them to stay in business, including workshops or other means of assisting licensed-exempt providers to become licensed. Agencies should work with providers to improve the quality of child care and to maintain and expand the number of child care providers available in the service area.

6.65 Administrative Issues of the Child Care Subsidy System

The child care subsidy system, whether it is operated by a public or private agency, should have written policies requiring integrity in fiscal management, internal fiscal controls regarding handling money, fraud financial accountability, accounting procedures, audits, and conflict of interest.

Administrative functions, including the time and efficiency of payment processes, can be improved and made more cost effective with the assistance of technology.

Agencies should strengthen their staff development programs to ensure that the staff in subsidy system programs are sensitive to issues of low-income families and understand the needs of working families. Eligibility counselors should have a bachelor's degree in social work or a related field.

7

Family Support, Social Services, and Mental Health Services

Goals

I. The child care service supports and strengthens the emotional and behavioral well-being of young children, especially where poverty or other environmental or biological risk factors have affected their development.

II. The child care service supports and assists parents in addressing the challenges that may interfere with their ability to promote their children's healthy emotional development.

III. The child care service strengthens the ability of teachers, caregivers, and providers to promote the emotional well-being of young children and families.

IV. The child care service ensures that young children with challenging behaviors and mental health issues have access to needed services and supports (Knitzer, 2000, p. 6).

Family Support and Social Services

Most parents who use child care services are able to manage their parental responsibilities well. They make child care arrangements because they want to or must work outside the home, complete their education, or obtain job training, or because they want their children to receive the benefit of the developmental, educational, social, health, and recreational experiences available in child care.

Some parents, however, experience challenges in planning for and using child care. These may include the physical or emotional illness of the child or parent; absence of an extended family or other support network; inexperience in parenting; substance abuse; or child abuse or neglect. The stress of these challenges, as well as circumstances such as homelessness, violence, poverty, and immigration status, can impede the capacity of parents to function, thereby weakening the family. Family support and social services offer support to parents seeking to cope with such challenges and to overcome their frequently adverse effects on the rearing and development of their children.

Mental Health Services

For most children, early childhood development proceeds smoothly; these children develop the kinds of emotional readiness and behavior skills that will help ensure that they enter school ready to succeed. But a significant number of young children are showing early signs of emotional distress and behavior problems. Many of these children may be unidentified, receive delayed diagnosis and treatment, or receive inappropriate or inadequate care.

Staff in a wide range of programs—Head Start, Early Head Start, child care, and home visiting programs—report great concern for these children, and often for their families. They say that their usual approaches often do not work, but they do not know where to turn to help. Many communities report that young children are being excluded from child care settings because of their behaviors. Other research indicates that early emotional and behavioral problems are either ignored or misidentified.*

Recent research provides hope for the increasing number of children served within child care settings who are experiencing emotional and behavioral problems. Child care services can play a key role by providing these children and their families with the developmentally responsive services and supports needed. This is done through building on their assets, both internal (support, empowerment, boundaries and expectations, constructive use of time) and external (commitment to learning, positive values, social competencies, and positive identity). When children are provided with services and programming that build on these assets, they have a greater capacity to succeed in school and to do better later in life (Search Institute, 2004b).

For some children, this is not enough. They may require the services of a qualified mental health professional who can provide services and supports to them on an individual basis, working with their parents, child care staff, and providers to understand and provide supports as well as enhancing the overall program in the child care setting. Research on effective mental health services has shown that integrating a mental health consultant into the program helps children who have an emotional or behavioral problem and who need more than what is offered through the child care service to achieve better outcomes (Knitzer, 2000).

---

* Most studies estimate the prevalence of psychopathology in children to be between 10 and 20% and suggest that rates may be rising with each generation. Fewer than 30% of children who have a mental disorder actually receive services from a qualified mental health professional. There have been relatively few studies of preschoolers but those that exist demonstrate that mental disorders occur at a similar frequency (up to 1 in 5 children). These disorders are persistent over time, with developmental consequences into later childhood, adolescence and adult life. In contrast to psychiatric disorders presenting later in childhood, those seen in preschoolers are likely to be closely related to somatic development, to language and social development, and to the child's relationships to parents and other caregivers (Blackwell, 1994; Fombonne, 2004; Knitzer, 2000, pp. 4–5).

7.1   Need for Family Support, Social Services, and Mental Health Services

Family support, social services, and mental health services should be an integral component of the child care service, providing help to those parents and children who may benefit from such supports and services.

The family support worker, social worker, or mental health therapist, either as staff or as a consultant, can use the knowledge and skills acquired through professional education and experience to:

- work with parents who need help in fulfilling their parental role, and help them to deal with problems that may affect their relationship to their children and their children's development;

- identify special needs or social, emotional, and health problems of the child or the family;

- provide strengths-based counseling services to parents under stress, and make referrals to the appropriate service provider for those families that require services beyond those provided by the family support worker, social worker, or mental health therapist;

- arrange for children to be screened and assessed by a qualified mental health professional for diagnosis and services when children with emotional and behavioral problems do not respond to the regular programming of the child care service;

- work with the child directly;

- help child care staff members and family child care providers understand the individualized needs of the child and family and how to best to work with them;

- work with the child care staff and family child care providers to design classroom environments and interventions to promote emotional strengths and strong relationships and to develop the skills for effectively dealing with any risk factors such as poverty, parental mental illness, or substance abuse (Knitzer, 2000, p. 7; Search Institute, 2004a);

- increase child care staff and family child care provider competencies in dealing with children with challenging behaviors or problematic emotional developments (Knitzer, 2000, p. 7);
- coordinate the delivery of family support, social services, and mental health services in the child care service;
- help parents obtain and use other community resources and services and help coordinate the different services a family may need; and
- help parents and children make a successful transition to the next step in the child's developmental care.

7.2 Providing Continuing Family Support, Social Services, and Mental Health Services to Children

The family support worker, social worker, or mental health therapist, either as a member of the child care service staff or as a consultant, should be available to the children in care throughout their use of the service.

The worker/therapist should have the skills and training needed to identify challenging behaviors and problematic emotional development in children. The worker/therapist may assist the child in identifying and coping with issues related to separation from parents, school, neighborhood friends, being in a new and unfamiliar environment, and conflicting behavioral expectations between program and home.

The worker/therapist should be aware of any cultural differences between the family and the child care service. The family support, social services, or mental health services should be provided in the language commonly used by the family.

The worker/therapist should work with the parents or the teacher/caregiver to help the children resolve problems that may impede their ability to successfully care for their children.

The worker/therapist may offer support to parents of children with special needs. One way to be of help is to link parents with others who have children with special needs. The worker/therapist can also help other parents and staff members become more accepting of children with special needs.

In addition to direct assistance when indicated, the worker/therapist should be prepared to make referrals to appropriate community resources and coordinate services for all children, including children with special needs. When the child has identified mental health needs, a qualified mental health care professional may provide the services and supports onsite/within the program or may assist the family in obtaining services such as psychiatric services, medication evaluation and monitoring, and psychological testing.

7.3   Providing Continuing Family Support, Social Services, and Mental Health Services to Parents

The worker/therapist, either as a member of the child care service staff or as a consultant, should be available to parents throughout their child's use of the service.

The worker/therapist may be called on:

- to support child care staff members and family child care providers in providing or arranging group services for parents such as family life education, parenting education, and parent support groups;
- for counseling services or guidance on child development or child rearing;
- to help parents prepare their children for any significant changes that may take place in their homes;
- to help parents cope with the stresses that can develop with difficulties of carrying a job, managing a home, and maintaining the energy to meet their child's needs; and
- to provide support when parents feel unprepared or inadequate in meeting their child's needs.

When needed, the worker/therapist should help parents to:

- recognize and deal realistically with special problems their child may be experiencing, as well as with their own anxieties or feelings in relation to their child's difficulties;

- turn to a child care staff member or family child care provider to help them with a particular concern;
- obtain practical help in child rearing, nutrition, and use of community resources; and
- accept referral to a community resource for problems requiring additional or specialized help.

A summary of the work of the worker/therapist with the parents should be included regularly in the child care record.

7.4   The Family Support Worker, Social Worker, or Mental Health Therapist as a Team Member of the Child Care Service

The worker/therapist, either as a member of the child care service staff or as a consultant, should function as a member of the child care service team. This includes:

As a member of the child care service team, the worker/therapist may:

- consult, with permission from the family, with other professionals and service providers, including the primary health care provider, who have had significant interaction with the family, regarding health and behavioral status, needs, and treatment plan;
- help the child care service staff understand child-parent relationships, the dynamics of child behavior and motivation, the effect of child care on the family, and the personal feelings that can affect staff member's relationships with the children or parents;
- learn how the child is getting along at home, in the neighborhood, at school, and in the child care program by means of observations, conferences with teachers/caregivers, and discussions with parents and others who know the child;
- help parents and teacher/caregivers give continuity and consistency to the care a child receives;
- provide consultation and advice to the child care staff on specific children who exhibit challenging behavior or have difficulties emotionally;

- work with the teachers/caregivers to design classroom interventions to identify and promote emotional strengths;
- provide training and support to improve the child care staff's competency when working with children with mental health needs;
- ensure that the child care service plays a part in the implementation of any treatment plan for children in its care who require mental health treatment, and, when the child's treatment is provided by an outside mental health practitioner, maintain a close working relationship with that provider; and
- work with the child care service to ensure that children and families are referred to community services when there are emotional or behavioral issues that are impacting their participation in the child care service.

The child care service should be prepared to help parents arrange for and access the needed mental health services.

7.5 Providing Continuing Family Support, Social Services, and Mental Health Services to Family Child Care and Group Child Care Providers

The worker/therapist should provide continuing support, as needed, to family child care and group child care providers throughout the time the children are receiving care in their homes.

Support should be given in the following areas:

- understanding and meeting the needs of the individual child or children in their home;
- dealing with problems as they arise;
- maintaining relationships with the child's parents and the child care service; and
- evaluating the usefulness of the family child care and group child care home for the particular needs of a given child and parents and the suitability of that home to provide the service, if necessary.

The worker/therapist should be responsive to parents and providers when problems are indicated and should provide individual counseling when appropriate.

The worker/therapist should help the provider relate the child's daily experiences to those in the child's home. The worker/therapist plays a vital role in facilitating the exchange of information and interaction between the provider and the child's parents.

The worker/therapist should help both the parents and the provider to better understand the difficulty children may encounter in adjusting to two families approaches, including differences in discipline, standards, and values.

The worker/therapist should support providers in better understanding the behavior of children and parents, managing challenging behavior, and dealing with their own feelings of anger or discouragement in the face of difficult situations.

The worker/therapist should work, in coordination with the primary health care provider, with the family child care providers to design interventions to identify and promote the emotional strengths of the children in the family child care or group family child care home.

The worker/therapist should provide training and support to improve the family child care provider's competency when working with children with mental health needs.

The worker/therapist should ensure, in coordination with the primary health care provider, that the family child care home play a part in the implementation of any treatment plan for children in its care who require mental health treatment. When the child's treatment involves an outside mental health practitioner, the family child care provider should maintain a close working relationship with that practitioner.

The worker/therapist should work with the family child care provider to ensure that children and families are referred to community services when there are emotional or behavioral issues that are impacting their participation in child care. The family child care provider should be prepared to help parents arrange for and access the needed mental health services.

Glossary

Administration—The people responsible for the provider's management functions, including fiscal and personnel resources, and service delivery. Such people determine provider goals, acquire and allocate resources to carry out a program, coordinate activities toward goal achievement, and monitor, evaluate, and make needed changes in processes and procedures to improve the likelihood of goal achievement.

Administrator—The person most responsible for the onsite, ongoing, daily supervision of the program and staff. The terms *administrator* and *director* are used interchangeably throughout these materials.

Admission—The child or youth's physical entry into or arrival at the provider's facility or program.

Age Groups—In the accreditation system, the following age groups are defined:

- Babies: Children from birth to 12 months. This term is used instead of *infants* because it conveys more warmth and is more commonly used by parents and providers.

- Toddlers: Children from 12 months through 2 years of age (35 months). *Younger toddlers* are defined as 12–17 months in age and *older toddlers* as 18–35 months in age.

- Preschool-Age Children: Children between the ages of 3 and 5.

- School-Age Children: Children between the ages of 6 and 12.

Agency—Public or private child welfare agencies or other organizations providing child care, development, and education services, including community-based organizations.

Assessment—To engage the child, youth, and family in identifying their needs, strengths, and resources to ascertain what services, if any, will be most helpful to them in addressing current concerns. The initial assessment should validate and augment the information obtained during referral and intake, and should provide the basis for establishing, with the child, youth, and family, measurable, realistic, achievable, and time-limited service objectives. The assessment should include the observations of the child, youth, and family and should show consideration of their cultural and ethnic perspectives. The assessment should be updated continuously throughout the service delivery process.

Attachment—A child's connection to a parent or other caregiver that endures over time, establishes an interpersonal connection, and aids in the development of a sense of self.

Attention Deficit Disorder (ADD)/Attention-Deficit/Hyperactivity Disorder (ADHD)—Neurobiological condition diagnosed in children, adolescents, and adults that encompasses a cluster of symptoms, including hyperactivity, impulsivity, short attention span, overarousal, and difficulty understanding long-term goals. When hyperactivity is not present, referred to as ADD. Both ADD and ADHD are extremely complex disorders of childhood that cause or exacerbate social, emotional, and school-related problems. Also called hyperactivity and hyperkinesis.

Autism—A disorder of the brain marked by a series of striking deviations from normal developmental patterns that manifest as disturbances in behavior, cognition, interpersonal communication, and social interactions.

Background Checks—The process of checking for history of criminal charges of potential child care providers before they are allowed to care for children.

Behavior Support—Behavior support includes the whole spectrum of activities from proactive and planned use of the environment, routines, and structure of the particular setting to less restrictive interventions such as positive reinforcement, verbal interventions, de-escalation techniques, and therapeutic activities that are conducive to each child's development of positive behavior.

Behavior Support Plan—A written document developed prior to or at admission that addresses the holistic needs of the child and includes the child's coping strategies, de-escalation preferences, and preferred intervention methods.

Best Practices—Recommended services, supports, interventions, policies, or procedures based on current validated research or expert consensus.

Bonding—Process through which a parent or other caregiver develops an emotional connection to a child.

Caregiver—Used here to indicate the primary staff who work directly with the children, that is, director, teacher, aide, or others in the center and the child care provider in small and large family child care homes.

Caseload—All individuals (usually counted as children or families) for whom a worker is responsible, as expressed in a ratio of clients to staff members.

Case Management Services—Help people and families achieve or maintain optimum social, psychological, and physical functioning by planning, securing, coordinating, and monitoring services from different organizations and personnel in behalf of those served (from the Council on Accreditation).

Center—A facility that provides care and education for any number of children in a nonresidential setting and is open on a regular basis (for example, it is not a drop-in facility).

Child Protective Services (CPS)—A process beginning with the assessment of a report of child abuse and neglect. If it is determined that the child is at risk of or has been abused or neglected, then CPS includes the provision of services and supports to the child and his or her family by the public child protection agency, a community agency or entity, or both.

Child-to-Staff Ratio—The maximum number of children permitted per caregiver. See also *Ratio*.

Child Well-Being—The healthy physical, emotional, intellectual, and spiritual development of a child. Child well-being is achieved when the following universal needs are met for each child:

- "The Basics": Basic needs such as proper nutrition, economic security, adequate shelter and clothing, education, and primary and preventive health and mental health care.
- Relationships: Nurturing relationships with parents, kin, and other adults and children.
- Opportunities: Opportunities for optimal development.
- Safety: Protection from harm.
- Healing: Easing the effects of harm (Morgan et al., 2003).

Child Welfare—The collective and necessary social and familial protections and provisions that should be provided all children and adolescents to assure their health, education, socialization, social membership, opportunities, and fair "life chances" (Brown & Weil, 1992).

Child Welfare Services—Child welfare services include a continuum of services ranging from prevention and intervention to treatment, for the purpose of protecting children, strengthening families to successfully care for their children, providing permanency when children cannot remain with their families, and promoting children's well-being. Services should be family centered, strengths based, and respectful of the family's cultures, values, beliefs, and needs.

Child Welfare System—The child welfare system includes elements of formal service delivery systems designed to ensure safety, achieve permanency for children, strengthen families to successfully care for their children, and promote the well-being and optimal development of children.

Collaboration—A process of individuals and organizations in a community working together toward a common purpose. All parties have a contribution to and a stake in the outcome.

Community—A group of individuals or families that share certain values, services, institutions, interests, or geographic proximity.

Confidentiality—The protection of information obtained during a services intervention from release to organizations or individuals not entitled to it by law or policy.

Counseling Services—Support personal growth and development and situational change by helping individuals and families cope with the stresses of daily living and manage psycho-social adjustments related to normal life cycle issues. Counseling services may also be provided in response to, or in conjunction with, other more intensive services to address such issues as victim traumas, substance abuse, job loss, depression, or medical illness (adapted from COA, 2001).

Cultural Competence—The ability of individuals and systems to respond respectfully and effectively to people of all cultures, classes, races, ethnic backgrounds, sexual orientations, and faiths or religions in a manner that recognizes, affirms, and values the worth of individuals, families, tribes, and communities, and protects and preserves the dignity of each.

De-escalation—The process of calming and reducing agitation and anxiety.

Developmental Delay—Delay in a child's physical, emotional, or mental development, such as a delay in language or gross motor development, that may or may not be open to remediation.

Developmental Disability—A childhood condition, disease, genetic disorder, growth pattern, or inability to meet developmental milestones that begins before 18 years of age, impairs the individual's functioning, and usually persists throughout the life of the individual (e.g., mental retardation, autism, cerebral palsy).

Developmental Disorder—Physical or mental handicap originating before the age of 18 that either is specific, such as a developmental reading, arithmetic, or language disorder, or pervasive, such as infantile autism.

Developmentally Appropriate Practices—This phrase refers to program methods and goals that respond to the ages, developmental stages, and individual differences of children and youth. A child's interests and abilities change as he or she grows and matures. Research suggests that these changes usually occur in a series of predictable stages. The changes often affect a child's social, physical, emotional, and intellectual needs. It is important for school-age staff to understand the stages of development as well as the individual needs of children. Such knowledge will help staff relate to every person in the program. It will also help the staff plan activities that are well suited to children and youth at different stages of development.

Disclosure—The act of revealing information that may be considered secret or confidential.

Early Childhood—Birth through age 8.

Emotional Maltreatment—Parental or other caregiver acts or omissions, such as rejecting, terrorizing, berating, ignoring, or isolating a child, that cause, or are likely to cause, serious impairment of the physical, social, mental, or emotional capacities of the child.

Evaluation—Impressions and recommendations formed after a careful appraisal and study.

Facility—The buildings, grounds, equipment, and people involved in providing child care of any type.

Family—Defined broadly to include circumstances in which a child may have one or more families simultaneously—for example, as a result of parental separation or divorce, open adoption of a child, or when a child is living with kin or in foster care. The term also includes a variety of family formations, including single-parent and blended families. Family may include birth or adoptive parents, grandparents, siblings, foster parents, legal guardians, or any other person in a parental role. Successful providers try to recognize and value the child's definition of family, even if it is different from the provider's experience.

Family-Centered Practice—A way of working with families, both formally and informally, across service systems, to enhance the capacity of families to provide care and protection for their children. It recognizes the strengths of family relationships and builds on these strengths to achieve optimal outcomes for children and families.

Family-Centered Services—A constellation of services that employ the family-centered practice approach and are provided in a number of settings and to meet a variety of family needs.

Family Child Care (FCC)—Family child care is offered in the provider's home for children from infancy through the school-age years. Many providers have their own children or relative in their family child care programs.

Family Foster Care—Essential child welfare service for children and their parents who must live apart from each other for a temporary period of time because of physical abuse, sexual abuse, neglect, or special circumstances. Children are placed in the homes of licensed, trained caregivers.

Family Resource, Support, and Education Services—Community-based services that assist and support parents in their role as caregivers, with the goal of promoting parental competencies and strengthening family life, leading to healthy child and family development.

Fetal Alcohol Effect/Fetal Alcohol Syndrome—Various forms of damage to an unborn infant due to heavy prenatal alcohol consumption. Potential problems include retarded growth, mental retardation, and sometimes craniofacial and limb abnormalities.

Group Size (also "Group")—The number of children assigned to a caregiver or team of caregivers occupying an individual classroom or well-defined space in a larger room. The group may gather for active games, team sports, group meetings, etc. More than one group may be engaged in an activity at the same time. For example, groups may be playing on the playground, watching a performance, or riding a bus. In general, group size and makeup will keep changing because of new activity choices or to meet the needs of individual children. Whenever possible, group sizes should not exceed 30 children. See also *Child-to-Staff Ratio*.

Hyperactivity—General restlessness or excessive muscular activity, frequently associated with internal tension or a neurological disorder and often marked by rapid movements, restlessness, and almost constant motion. An informal term sometimes used to refer to attention-deficit/hyperactivity disorder. See also *Attention Deficit Disorder (ADD)/Attention Deficit/ Hyperactivity Disorder (ADHD)*.

Infant—A child between the time of birth and the age of ambulation (usually between the ages from birth to 18 months).

Institutional Abuse—Maltreatment of children or vulnerable adults while they are being cared for in settings outside the child's home.

Intake—The process during which a child, youth, or family's eligibility to receive services is assessed in comparison to the provider's established criteria.

Investigation—An inquiry or search by law enforcement and CPS to determine the validity of a report of child abuse or neglect or to determine if a crime has been committed.

Juvenile and Family Courts—Established in states to handle legal matters concerning juveniles. Most often they have jurisdiction over child abuse and neglect, status offenders, and juvenile delinquency. In some states, they also have jurisdiction over domestic violence, divorce, child custody, and child support.

Kindergartners—Children in first year of formal schooling, usually 5 to 6 years old. Children in kindergarten are considered preschoolers in these materials.

Kinship Care—The full-time nurturing and protection of children by relatives, members of their tribes or clans, godparents, stepparents, or other adults who have a kinship bond with a child.

Large Family Child Care Home—Usually, care and education for 7 to 12 children (including preschool children of the caregiver) in the home of the caregiver, who employs one or more qualified adult assistants to meet the child-to-staff ratio requirements. This type of care is likely to resemble center care in its organization of activities. Applicable terms are abbreviated here to *large family home* or *large family home caregiver.*

Learning Disability—Psychologically or organically based difficulty in learning such basic skills as reading, writing, and arithmetic affecting children of normal or above-average intelligence. Also called *learning disorder.*

Loss—Emotional and psychological state experienced when a person is temporarily or permanently separated from someone or something important in his or her life.

Mandated Reporter—A person who in his or her professional capacity is required by state or provincial law to report suspected child abuse or neglect to the designated state or provincial agency. In some states, all adults are mandated to report suspected child abuse or neglect.

Medically Fragile—Term used to describe a child with one or more severe medical problems (e.g., HIV/AIDS, prenatal alcohol or drug exposure).

Monitoring—Third-party, objective observation of physical interventions to assess and ensure that the intervention is performed according to procedure and that the child's physical and psychological well-being are maintained.

Multidisciplinary Team—A group established among agencies or individuals to promote collaboration and shared decision-making around the protection of children. Some multidisciplinary teams address issues related to individual children and families, whereas others focus more on community-wide prevention and protection strategies.

Neglect—Failure of parents or other caregivers, for reasons not solely due to poverty, to provide the child with needed age-appropriate care, including food, clothing, shelter, protection from harm, supervision appropriate to the child's development, hygiene, education, and medical care.

Out-of-Home Care—Array of services, including family foster care, kinship care, and group residential care, for children who have been placed in the custody of the state and who must reside temporarily away from their families.

Parent—The child's birth or adoptive mother or father, guardian, or other legally responsible person, which may include grandparents, foster parents, and same-gender co-parents.

Permanency Planning—Process through which planned and systematic efforts are made to assure that children are in safe and nurturing family relationships expected to last a lifetime.

Physical Abuse—Physical acts by parents or other caregivers that cause, or could have caused, physical injury to the child.

Policies—Written requirements that direct the business and service-delivery practices within the provider. They should carry the approval of the provider's governing or advisory board.

Preschooler—A child between the age of toilet learning/training and the age of entry into a regular school; usually ages 3 to 5 years and related to overall development. Children in kindergarten are considered preschoolers in these materials.

Procedures—Written guidelines developed by the provider's administration to ensure that provider practice is consistent with board-approved policies.

Program—Part-day and full-day group programs in schools and other facilities serving a minimum of 10 children from birth through age 5 or school-age children before or after school. The terms *center* and *program* are used interchangeably throughout this document.

Provider—Any facility, organization, agency, institution, program, or person that provides services to children. In general, *provider* means an organization, whereas *caregiver* refers to an individual. In some settings, the provider and caregiver may be a single person. NAFCC accreditation requires the provider to be onsite and actively involved at least 80% of the time care is offered. When a standard refers to the *provider*, the term also applies to the co-provider, assistant, or substitute.

Ratio—Ratio refers to the number of staff at the program compared to the number of children enrolled. Low ratios ensure that there are enough staff to maintain the safety and security of the children. Appropriate ratios also help create an environment where children feel emotionally secure. When there are enough adults to supervise a given group, the staff-to-child interactions can be more meaningful. Recommended licensing ratios vary from one state to the next. The numbers may be slightly higher or lower than the NSACA ratios for accreditation. The minimum ratios that must be met to achieve NSACA accreditation vary according to the ages and abilities of children. The ratio is between 1:10 and 1:15 for groups of children age 6 and older. The ratio is between 1:8 and 1:12 for groups that include children younger than 6.

Respite Care—Temporary relief provided to primary caregivers to reduce stress, support family stability, prevent abuse and neglect, and minimize the need for out-of-home placement or placement disruption.

School-Age Care Program—School-age care program refers to an organization that provides care for children and youth between the ages of 5 and 14 during their out-of-school time. Successful school-age programs work in cooperation with families to provide guidance, supervision, and support to the individuals in their care.

School-Age Child—This term describes a developmental period associated with a child who is enrolled in a regular school, including kindergarten, usually from ages 5 to 12 years.

School-Age Child Care Facility—A center offering a program of activities before and after school or during vacations.

School-Age Children—Children attending first grade or beyond who are participating in a before- or afterschool program.

Separation Anxiety—Fear experienced by an individual when confronted with the potential temporary or permanent loss of a caregiver.

Service Plan—A written plan of action, usually developed between the family, child, social worker, and other service providers. It identifies needs, sets goals, and describes strategies and timelines for achieving goals.

Sexual Abuse—Sexual activity by a parent or other caregiver with a child, including, but not limited to, any kind of sexual contact through persuasion, physical force, or other coercive means; exploitation through sexual activity that is allowed, encouraged, or coerced; and child prostitution or pornography.

Sibling—An individual who is a brother or sister to another child through a birth or adoptive relationship.

Single-Parent Family—Family unit comprising a mother or a father, but not both, and at least one child.

Small Family Child Care Home—Usually, the care and education of one to six children (including preschool children of the caregiver) in the home of the caregiver. Caregivers model their programs either on a nursery school or on a skilled parenting model. Applicable terms are abbreviated here to *small family home* or *family home caregiver*.

Small Family Child Care Home Network—A group of small family child care homes in one management system.

Social Work—The professional activity of helping individuals, groups, or communities to enhance or restore their capacity for social functioning and creating societal conditions favorable to this goal.

Social Work Practice—The professional application of social work values, principles, and techniques toward achievement of one or more of the following ends:

- helping people obtain tangible services;
- counseling with individuals, families, or groups;
- helping communities or groups provide or improve social and health services; and

• participating in the legislative process.

The practice of social work requires knowledge of human development and behavior; social, economic, and cultural institutions; and the interaction of these factors.

Special Needs—Children with developmental disabilities, mental retardation, emotional disturbance, sensory or motor impairment, or significant chronic illness who require special health surveillance or specialized programs, interventions, technologies, or facilities.

Staff—All personnel employed at the facility, including both caregivers and personnel who do not provide direct care to the children (such as cooks, drivers, and housekeepers).

Targeted Behavior—A behavior identified in the child's individualized service plan as the behavior needing to be modified or eliminated. Targeted behaviors should be observable and measurable.

Teaching Staff—Paid adults who have direct responsibilities for the care and education of the children.

Time-Out—A strategy used to teach individuals to calm themselves, during which a child is not given the opportunity to receive positive reinforcement or participate in the current routine or activity until he or she is less agitated. The length of the time-out interval should be short and based on the individual's developmental level, limited to the period necessary for the individual to calm down. The criteria for ending the time-out should be communicated to the individual.

Toddler—A child between the age of ambulation and the age of toilet learning/training, usually one ages 13 to 35 months.

Training Program—A provider's comprehensive training program that may include the provider's inservice training, training provided by an external trainer, and staff attendance at external training.

Trauma-Informed Care—Delivery of services in a manner that seeks to identify and consider each individual's trauma history, is appropriate to the special needs of trauma survivors, understands and accommodates the vulnerabilities of trauma survivors, and avoids retraumatization.

Universal Precautions—These apply to blood and other body fluids containing blood, semen, and vaginal secretions, but not to feces, nasal secretions, sputum, sweat, tears, urine, saliva, and vomitus unless they contain visible blood or are likely to contain blood. Universal precautions include avoiding injuries caused by sharp instruments or devices and the use of protective barriers such as gloves, gowns, aprons, masks, or protective eyewear, which can reduce the risk of exposure of the worker's skin or mucous membranes that could come in contact with materials that may contain blood-borne pathogens while the worker is providing first aid or care.

Workload—The amount of work required to successfully manage a case and bring it to resolution. It is based on the responsibilities assigned to complete a specific task, or set of tasks, for which the social worker is responsible.

Selected References

Acs, G., Phillips, K. R., & McKenzie, D. (2000). *Playing by the rules but losing the game: America's working poor.* Available from http://www.urban.org/content/IssuesInFocus/TheWorkingPoor/Reports/Reports.htm. Washington, DC: Urban Institute.

Adams, G., & Snyder, K. (2003). *Child care subsidy policies and practices: Implications for child care providers.* Washington, DC: Urban Institute.

Benard, B. (1999). The foundations of the resiliency framework: From research to practice. In N. Henderson, B. Benard, & N. Sharp-Light (Eds.), *Resiliency in action: Practical ideas for overcoming risks and building strengths in youth, families, & communities.* San Diego, CA: Resiliency in Action.

Bess, R., Andrews, C., Jantz, A., Russell, V., & Geen, R. (2002). *The cost of protecting vulnerable children III: What factors affect states' fiscal decisions?* Washington, DC: Urban Institute.

Better Baby Care. (n.d.). *How to get involved.* Available from http://www.betterbabycare.org/involved.html.

Bond, J. T., Galinsky, E. & Swanberg, J. E. (1998). *1997 national study of the changing workforce* (Executive summary). New York: Families and Work Institute.

Bowlby, J. (1973). *Attachment and loss—Vol. III: Separation.* New York: Basic Books.

Cahan, E. D. (1989). *Past caring: A history of U.S. preschool care and education for the poor, 1820–1965.* New York: National Center for Children in Poverty, Columbia University.

Capizzano, J., & Adams, G. (2000). *The number of child care arrangements used by children under five: Variation across states.* Washington, DC: Urban Institute.

Carolina Abecedarian Project. (1999). *Gains from high quality child care persist into adulthood—Landmark study.* Available from www.fpg.unc.edu.

Centers for Disease Control and Prevention. (2001). *Web-based injury statistics query and reporting system (WISQARS)*. Atlanta, GA: Centers for Disease Control and Prevention, National Center for Injury Prevention and Control.

Child Welfare League of America. (2002). *Cultural competence agency self-assessment instrument*. Washington, DC: CWLA Press.

Child Welfare League of America. (1988). *CWLA standards for the health care of children in out-of-home care*. Washington, DC: Author.

Child Welfare League of America. (1989). *CWLA standards for independent-living services*. Washington, DC: Author.

Child Welfare League of America. (1995). *CWLA standards of excellence for family foster care services*. Washington, DC: Author.

Child Welfare League of America. (1996). *CWLA Standards of excellence for the management and governance of child welfare organizations*. Washington, DC: Author.

Child Welfare League of America. (1998). *CWLA Standards of excellence for adolescent pregnancy prevention, pregnant adolescents, and young parents*. Washington, DC: Author.

Child Welfare League of America. (1999). *CWLA standards of excellence for services for abused or neglected children and their families*. Washington, DC: Author.

Child Welfare League of America. (2000a). *2000 membership trends and issues survey*. Washington, DC: Author.

Child Welfare League of America. (2000b). *CWLA standards for adoption services*. Washington, DC: Author.

Child Welfare League of America. (2000c). *CWLA standards for kinship care services*. Washington, DC: Author.

Child Welfare League of America. (2001). *The child welfare workforce challenge: Results from a preliminary study*. Washington, DC: Author.

Child Welfare League of America. (2002a). *Cultural competence*. Available from http://www.cwla.org/programs/culturalcompetence. Washington, DC: Author.

Child Welfare League of America. (2002b). *CWLA best practice guidelines for behavior management*. Washington, DC: Author.

Child Welfare League of America. (2002c). *Research roundup: Child welfare workforce*. Washington, DC: Author.

Child Welfare League of America. (2004). *CWLA standards for residential care services*. Washington, DC: Author.

Children's Defense Fund. (2000). *Families struggling to make it in the workforce: A post welfare report*. Available from http://www.childrensdefense.org/pdf/CMPreport.pdf. Washington, DC: Author.

Children's Foundation. (2003). *Children's Foundation child care licensing study*. Washington, DC: Author.

Cole, E., Day, P., & Steppe, S. (1994). *Report of the CWLA family strengths project*. Unpublished report.

Council on Accreditation for Children and Family Services. (2001). *Standards and self-study manual* (7th Ed.). New York: Author.

Cross, T. L. (1998). Understanding family resiliency from a relational world view. In H. I. McCubbin, E. A. Thompson, A. I. Thompson, & J. E. Fromer (Eds.), *Resiliency in Native American and immigrant families* (pp. 143–157). Thousand Oaks, CA: Sage.

Dicker, S., Gordon, E., & Knitzer, J. (2001). *Improving the odds for the healthy development of young children in foster care*. New York: National Center for Children in Poverty.

Drais-Parrillo, A. (2002). *2001 salary study*. Washington, DC: CWLA Press.

Egley, A., Jr. (2002). *National Youth Gang Survey trends from 1996 to 2000*. Washington, DC: Office of Juvenile Justice and Delinquency Prevention.

Egley, A., Jr. & Arjunan, M. (2002). *Highlights of the 2000 National Youth Gang Survey*. Washington, DC: Office of Juvenile Justice and Delinquency Prevention.

Ehrle, J., Geen, R., & Clark, R. (2001). *Children cared for by relatives: Who are they and how are they faring?* Washington, DC: Urban Institute.

Federal Interagency Forum on Child and Family Statistics. (2002). *America's children: Key national indicators of well-being, 2002*. Washington, DC: U.S. Government Printing Office.

Field, J., & Casper, L. M. *America's families and living arrangements: March 2000* (pp. 20–537). Washington, DC: U.S. Bureau of the Census.

FitzPatrick, C. S., & Campbell, N. D. (2002, November). *The little engine that hasn't*. Washington, DC: National Women's Law Center.

Gable, S. (2002, July). *Nature, nurture, and early brain development*. Available from http://www.classbrain.com/cb_pta/missouri_pdfs/kidsbrains.pdf.

Gardner, H. (1983). *Frames of mind*. New York: Basic Books.

Garner, B. A. (Ed.). (1999). *Black's law dictionary* (7th ed.). St. Paul, MN: West Group.

George, R. M., & Lee, B. J. (1997). Abuse and neglect of children. In R. A. Maynard (Ed.), *Kids having kids: Economic costs and social consequences of teen pregnancy* (pp. 205–230). Washington, DC: Urban Institute Press.

Gil, D. G. (1970). *Violence against children*. Cambridge, MA: Harvard University Press.

Gish, M. (2002, March). *Child care: Funding and spending under federal block grants.* Congressional Research Service.

Goldstein, J., Freud, A., & Solnit, A. J. (1973). *Beyond the best interests of the child.* New York: Free Press.

Green, J. W. (1999). *Cultural awareness in the human services: A multiethnic approach.* Needham Heights, MA: Allyn and Bacon.

Hawley, T. (2000). *Starting smart: How early experiences affect brain development* (2nd ed.). Chicago: Ounce of Prevention Fund and Zero to Three.

Head Start Bureau. (2003, February). Head Start program fact sheet. Available from http:/www.acf.dhhs.gov/programs/hsb/research/2003.htm.

Hill, R. B. (1999). *The strengths of African-American families: Twenty-five years later.* Lanham, MD: University Press of America.

Hodges, V. G. (1995). *Supporting and preserving families: A strengths-based approach.* Presentation at the National Conference of the Child Welfare League of America, Washington, DC.

Immigration and Naturalization Service. (2003). *Estimates of the unauthorized immigrant population residing in the United States: 1990 to 2000, Executive summary.* Available from www.immigration.gov/graphics/shared/aboutus/statistics/Illegals.htm. Washington, DC: U.S. Department of Justice.

Internal Revenue Service. (2000, Fall). *Statistics of income bulletin. Table 2 individual income tax returns 2000.* Washington, DC: Author.

Kaplan, H. I., & Sadock, B. J. (1995). *Comprehensive textbook of psychiatry.* Philadelphia: Lippincott Williams & Wilkins.

Kinsey, S. J. (2001). *Multi-age grouping and academic achievement in elementary school.* Champaign, IL: Clearinghouse on Elementary and Early Childhood Education.

Knitzer, J. (2000). *Promoting resilience: Helping young children and parents affected by substance abuse, domestic violence, and depression in the context of welfare reform.* New York: National Center for Children in Poverty.

Lally, J. R., Griffin, A., Fenichel, E., Segal, M., Szanton, E., & Weissbourd, B. (2001). *Caring for infant and toddlers in groups: Developmentally appropriate practice.* Washington, DC: Zero to Three Center for Program Excellence.

Landsverk, J. (2000). Child welfare and identification of mental health needs. In *U.S. Public Health Service: Report of the Surgeon General's conference on children's mental health: A national action agenda.* Washington, DC: U.S. Department of Health and Human Services.

Leigh, J. W. (1998). *Communicating for cultural competence.* Needham Heights, MA: Allyn & Bacon.

Lennon, M. C., Blome, J., & English, K. (2001). *Depression and low-income women: Challenges for TANF and welfare to work policies and programs* (Executive summary). New York: National Center for Children in Poverty.

Llobrera, J. (2004, August 16). *Food stamp caseloads are rising.* Available from http://www.cbpp.org/1-15-02fa.htm. Washington, DC: Center on Budget and Policy Priorities.

Maas, H. S., & Engler, R. E., Jr. (1959). *Children in need of parents.* New York: Columbia University Press.

Martin, J. A., Hamilton, B. E., Ventura, S. J., Menacker, F., Park, M. M., & Sutton, P. D. (2002). Births: Final data for 2001. *National Vital Statistics Reports, 51*(2).

Maynard, R. A. (Ed.). (1996). *Kids having kids: A Robin Hood Foundation special report on the costs of adolescent childbearing.* New York: Robin Hood Foundation.

McAdoo, H. P. (1998). African-American families: Strengths and realities. In H. I. McCubbin, E. A. Thompson, A. I. Thompson, & J. A. Futrell (Eds.), *Resiliency in African-American families* (pp. 17–30). Thousand Oaks, CA: Sage.

McCart, L., & Bruner, C. (2003). *Child welfare and school readiness: Marking the link for vulnerable children.* Des Moines, IA: State Early Childhood Policy Technical Assistance Network.

McPhatter, A. R., & Ganaway, T. L. (2003, March/April). Beyond the rhetoric: Strategies for implementing culturally effective practice with children, families, and communities. *Child Welfare, 82,* 103–124.

Miller, O. A., & Gaston, R. J. (2003, March/April). A model of culture-centered child welfare practice. *Child Welfare, 82,* 235–250.

Missouri Department of Social Services. (1999). *In the interest of minds.* Jefferson City, MO: Kauffman Foundation.

Moeller, A. (2002). *Key elements of a quality family child care service.* Washington, DC: Child Welfare League of America.

Mordock, J. B. (2002). *Managing for outcomes.* Washington, DC: CWLA Press.

Morgan, L. J., Spears, L. S., & Kaplan, C. (2003). *Making children a national priority: A framework for community action.* Washington, DC: Author.

Mumola, C. J. (2000). *Incarcerated parents and their children.* Washington, DC: U.S. Department of Justice.

Nansel, T. R., Overpeck, M., Pilla, R. S., Ruan, W. J., Simons-Morton, B., & Scheidt, P. (April 25, 2001). Bullying behaviors among US youth: Prevalence and association with psychosocial adjustment. *Journal of the American Medical Association, 2*(16), 2094–2210.

Nash, K. A., & Velazquez, J., Jr. (2003). *Cultural competence: A guide for human service agencies* (Rev. ed.). Washington, DC: CWLA Press.

National Association of Child Care Resource and Referral Agencies. (2002). *Criteria for best practices in the delivery of consumer education and referral.* Washington, DC: Author.

National Association for Family Child Care. (2002). *Provider's self-study workbook: Quality standards for NAFCC accreditation* (3rd ed.) Spring Valley, CA: Author.

National Association for the Education of Young Children. (1998). *Accreditation criteria and procedures of the National Association for the Education of Young Children.* Washington, DC: Author.

National Association for the Education of Young Children. (2002, November). *Licensing policy position.* Available from http://www.naeyc.org.

National Center for Children in Poverty. (2000). *Promoting the emotional well-being of children and families: Using mental health strategies to move the early childhood agenda and promote school readiness.* New York: Carnegie Corporation.

National Center for Injury Prevention and Control. (2004). *Suicide: Fact sheet.* Available from http://www.cdc.gov/ncipc/factsheets/suifacts.htm.

National Child Care Information Center. (2002). *Tiered strategies: Quality rating, reimbursement, licensing.* Washington, DC: Author.

National Indian Child Welfare Association. (1996). *Cross-cultural skills in Indian child welfare: A guide for the non-Indian.* Portland, OR: Author.

National Institute of Out-of-School Time. (2003). *Making the case: A fact sheet on children and youth in out-of school time.* Washington, DC: Author.

National Mental Health Association. (2001). *Mental health statistics fact sheet.* Available from http://www.nmha.org/infotr/factsheet/15.cfm.

National Network for Family Resiliency. (1996). *Family resiliency: Building strengths to meet life's challenges.* Ames, IA: Author.

Nicholson, J., Biebel, K., Hinden, B., Henry, A., & Stier, L. (2001). *Critical issues for parents with mental illness and their families.* Rockville, MD: SAMHSA's National Mental Health Information Center.

Office of Applied Studies. (2003). *The NHSDA report: Children living with substance-abusing or substance-dependent parents.* Rockville, MD: Substance Abuse and Mental Health Services Administration.

Office of Juvenile Justice and Delinquency Prevention. (2002). *OJJDP statistical briefing book.* Available from http://ojjdp.ncjrs.org/ojstatbb/asp/JAR_Display.asp?ID=qa2200012002. Washington, DC: Author.

Osofsky, J. D. (1997). Children and youth violence: An overview of the issues. In J. D. Osofsky (Ed.), *Children in a violent society* (pp. 3–8). New York: Guilford Press.

Padilla, Y. C. (1997). Immigrant policy: Issues for social work practice. *Social Work, 42,* 595–606.

Parlakian, R., & Seibel, N. L. (2002). *Building strong foundations: Practical guidance for promoting the social-emotional development of infants and toddlers.* Washington, DC: Zero to Three Center for Program Excellence.

Peisner-Feinberg, E. S., Burchinal, M. L., Clifford, R. M., Yazejian, N., Culkin, M. L., Zelazo, J., et al. (1999). *The children of the cost, quality, and outcomes study go to school* (Executive Summary). Chapel Hill, NC: University of North Carolina.

Proctor, B. D., & Dalaker, J. (2002). *Poverty in the United States: 2001.* (Current Population Reports, P60–219). Washington, DC: U.S. Government Printing Office.

Quinn, K., & Epstein, M. H. (1998). Characteristics of children, youth, and families served by local interagency systems of care. In M. H. Epstein, K. Kutash, & A. Duchnowski (Eds.), *Outcomes for children and youth with emotional and behavioural disorders and their families* (pp. 81–114). Austin, TX: Pro-Ed.

Rennison, C. M. (2003). *Intimate partner violence, 1993–2001.* Washington, DC: U.S. Department of Justice.

Rennison, C. M., & Welchans, S. (2000). *Intimate partner violence.* Washington, DC: U.S. Department of Justice.

Reynolds, A. J., Wang, M. C., & Walberg, H. J. (Eds.). (2003). *Early childhood programs for a new century.* Washington, DC: Child Welfare League of America.

Rice, K. F., Burkes, J., & Kaplan-Sanoff, M. (2001). *Early literacy.* Available from http://www.zerotothree.org/brainwonders.

Richer, E., Rahmanou, H., & Greenberg, M. (2003). *Welfare caseloads increase in most states in fourth quarter.* Available from www.clasp.org/Pubs/Pubs_Welfare. Washington, DC: Center for Law and Social Policy.

Roberts, D. (2002). *Shattered bonds: The color of child welfare.* Boulder, CO: Perseus Group Books.

Roman, J. (Ed.) (1998). *The NSACA standards for quality school-age care.* Boston: National School-Age Care Alliance.

San Miguel, S. K., Morrison, G. M., & Weissglass, T. (1998). The relationship of sources of support and service needs: Resilience patterns in low-income Latino/Hispanic families. In H. I. McCubbin, E. A. Thompson, A. I. Thompson, & J. E. Fromer (Eds.), *Resiliency in Native American and immigrant families* (pp. 385–400). Thousand Oaks, CA: Sage.

Scannapieco, M., & Jackson, S. (1996). Kinship care: The African American response to family preservation. *Social Work, 41,* 190–196.

Schmidley, D. (2003). *The foreign-born population in the United States: March 2002* (Current Population Reports, Series P20-539). Washington, DC: U.S. Government Printing Office.

Schulman, K. (2000). *Issue brief: The high cost of child care puts quality care out of reach for many families.* Washington, DC: Children's Defense Fund.

Shonkoff, J. P., & Phillips, D. A. (Eds.). (2000). *From neurons to neighborhoods: The science of early childhood development* (Executive summary). Washington, DC: National Academy Press.

Silver, J., DiLorenzo, P., Zukoski, M., Ross, P. E., Amster, B. J., & Schlegel, D. (1999). Starting young: Improving the health and developmental outcomes of infants and toddlers in the child welfare system. *Child Welfare, 78,* 148–165.

Smith, B. J., & Fox, L. (2003, January). *Systems of service delivery: A synthesis of evidence relevant to young children at risk of or who have challenging behavior.* Tampa, FL: Center for Evidence-Based Practice: Young Children with Challenging Behavior.

Snyder, H. N. (2002). *Juvenile arrests, 2000.* Washington, DC: Office of Juvenile Justice and Delinquency Prevention.

Snyder, H. N., & Sickmund, M. (1999). *Juvenile offenders and victims: 1999 National report.* Washington, DC: Office of Juvenile Justice and Delinquency Prevention.

Sonenstein, F. L., Gates, G. J., Schmidt, S., & Bolshun, N. (2002). *Primary child care arrangements of employed parents: Findings from the 1999 National Survey of America's Families.* Washington, DC: Urban Institute.

Thompson, R. A. (1995). *Preventing child maltreatment through social support: A critical analysis.* Thousand Oaks, CA: Sage.

Torgan, C. (2002, June). *Childhood obesity on the rise.* Available from http://www.nih.gov/news/WordonHealth/jun2002/childhood obesity.htm.

Urban Institute. (2002). *Nearly 20.5 million children of employed parents in child care.* Available from http://www.urban.org/url.cfm?ID=900532.

U.S. Bureau of the Census. (2001). *Table MC1. Married couples by labor force status of spouses: 1986 to present.* Available from www.census.gov/population/www/socdemo/hh-fam.html. Washington, DC: Author.

U.S. Bureau of the Census. (2003a). *Statistical abstract of the United States: 2002.* Washington, DC: U.S. Government Printing Office.

U.S. Bureau of the Census. (2003b). *Table 2. General mobility, by race, Hispanic origin, sex, and age: March 2000-2001.* Available from http://www.census.gov/population/www/socdemo/migrate/cps2001.html. Washington, DC: Author.

U.S. Conference of Mayors. (2002). *A status report on hunger and homelessness in America's cities: 2002.* Available from http://www.usmayors.org/uscm/hungersurvey/2002/onlinereport/HungerAndHomelessReport2002.pdf.

U.S. Department of Agriculture. (1996). *Keeping kids safe: A guide for safe handling and sanitation for child care providers.* Washington, DC: U.S. Department of Agriculture.

U.S. Department of Health and Human Services. (1999). *Mental health: A report of the surgeon general.* Rockville, MD: Author.

U.S. Department of Health and Human Services. (2000). *Temporary Assistance for Needy Families (TANF) program: Third annual report to Congress.* Washington, DC: Author.

U.S. Department of Health and Human Services. (2001). *Youth violence: A report of the surgeon general.* Rockville, MD: U.S. Department of Health and Human Services, Centers for Disease Control and Prevention, National Center for Injury Prevention and Control, Substance Abuse and Mental Health Services Administration, Center for Mental Health Services, and National Institutes of Health and National Institute of Mental Health.

U.S. Department of Health and Human Services. (2002a). *Child welfare outcomes 1999: Annual report.* Washington, DC: U.S. Government Printing Office.

U.S. Department of Health and Human Services. (2002b). *Preliminary FY 2001 estimates as of March 2003 (The AFCARS Report).* Available from http://www.acf.hhs.gov/programs/cb/publications/afcars/report8.htm.

U.S. Department of Health and Human Services. (2003a). *Child maltreatment: 2001.* Washington, DC: U.S. Government Printing Office.

U.S. Department of Health and Human Services. (2003b). *Temporary Assistance for Needy Families Program (TANF): Fifth annual re-*

port to Congress. Available from www.acf.dhhs.gov/programs/ofa/ annualreport5/index.htm. Washington, DC: Author.

U.S. Department of Health and Human Services, Administration on Children, Youth and Families. (2003). *Child maltreatment 2001: Reports from the states to the National Child Abuse and Neglect Data System.* Washington, DC: U.S. Government Printing Office.

U.S. Department of Health and Human Services, Health Resources and Services Administration, Maternal and Child Health Bureau. (2002). *Caring for our children, national health and safety performance standards: Guidelines for out-of-home child care* (2nd ed.). Elk Grove Village, IL: American Academy of Pediatrics, American Public Health Association, National Resource Center for Health and Safety in Child Care.

U.S. Department of Health and Human Services, Public Health Service, Substance Abuse and Mental Health Services Administration, Center for Substance Abuse Treatment. (n.d.). *Report to Congress on the Treatment and Prevention of Co-Occurring Substance Abuse and Mental Health Disorders.* Washington, DC: Author.

U.S. General Accounting Office. (1994). *Residential care: Some high-risk youth benefit, but more study needed* (GAO/HEHS-94-56). Washington, DC: Author.

U.S. General Accounting Office. (2003). *Child welfare: HHS could play a greater role in helping child welfare agencies recruit and retain staff* (GAO-03-357). Washington, DC: Author.

U.S. Public Health Service. (2000). *Report of the Surgeon General's conference on children's mental health: A national action agenda.* Washington, DC: U.S. Department of Health and Human Services.

Vega, W. A. (1995). The study of Latino families: A point of departure. In R. E. Zambrana (Ed.), *Understanding Latino families: Scholarship, policy, and practice* (pp. 3–17). Thousand Oaks, CA: Sage.

Wolfe, B., & Perozek, M. (1997). Teen children's health and health care use. In R. A. Maynard (Ed.), *Kids having kids: Economic costs and social consequences of teen pregnancy* (pp. 181–203). Washington, DC: Urban Institute Press.

Wright, L. E., & Seymour, C. B. (2000). *Working with children and families separated by incarceration: A handbook for child welfare agencies.* Washington, DC: CWLA Press.

Young, N. K., Gardner, S. L., & Dennis, K. (1998). *Responding to alcohol and other drug problems in child welfare: Weaving together practice and policy.* Washington, DC: CWLA Press.

Index*

---

* Reference locators in **bold type** indicate page numbers. All other reference locators indicate standard sections.

the symptoms of shaken baby syndrome, 2.27; effects on early brain development, **26**; responsive for infants, 1.6. *See also* Teacher/care provider

Career ladder, for staff, 4.50

Caregiver, **215**, **222**

Caring for Our Children: National Health and Safety Performance Standards, 2.4, 3.9; Standard 5.180, 3.23; Standard 5.4, 3.23; Standards 3.042-3.044, 3.43; Standards 3.070-3.080, 2.16; Standards 4.013-4.020, 2.28

Case management services, **215**; providing supportive, 6.62

Caseload, **215**

Cause and effect, exploring for toddlers, 1.7

CCDBG (Child Care and Development Block Grant), **6**, **33**, 6.56

CCDF (Child Care and Development Fund), **7**

CDA (Child development associate) certification, 4.17

Ceilings, sound-absorbing in the playroom, 3.16

Center, **215**. *See also* Program

Center directors: responsibilities of, 4.7; skills required by, 4.8

Center-based care, 6.59

Center-based child care program, teacher/care provider responsibilities, 4.9–4.15

Central burner, in child care center buildings, 3.6

Central heating, for a child care center, 3.14

Challenging behaviors, management of, **30**

Changing surface, for diapers, 3.9, 3.30

Charities, funding or subsidies for child care, **34**

Chemical sterilization, of dishes, 3.7, 3.28

Chemicals, in a family or group child care home, 3.40

Chest x-rays, for staff, 2.16

Child abuse: confidentiality of information in cases, 5.18; policy on compliance with reporting laws, 5.17; prevention and identification of institutional, 2.25; registry information, 4.34; reporting, 6.41

Child and Adult Care Food Program, **33**

Child care: building a community-based system for, **34–37**; building a constituency for, **35**; children in multiple arrangements, **9**; cost of, **11**, **32**; federal funding streams for, **6**; federal spending on, **7**; funding of, **32–34**; licensing, 5.21; participation and facility data, **25**; planning for new facilities, **37**; range of financial support for, **32**; regulation of all forms of, 6.2; types of, 6.59

Child care aides: parents as, 5.19; responsibilities of, 4.19; skills required of, 4.20

Child Care and Development Block Grant (CCDBG), **6**, **33**, 6.56

Child Care and Development Fund (CCDF), **7**

Child care center(s), **25**, 6.59; numbered licensed, **25**; planning or building, 3.1–3.3

Child care center buildings, 3.4; diaper changing areas, 3.9; disposition of space in, 3.8; external environment for, 3.5; handwashing facilities, 3.9; kitchen facilities, 3.10; lighting, 3.15; meetings space, 3.11; outdoor play area, 3.20–3.24; play space, 3.13–3.19; ratio of playroom floor space per child, 3.13; reception room, 3.11; sanitation requirements for, 3.7; staff office space, 3.11; structure and safety of, 3.6; toilet facilities, 3.9

Child care developmental learning program, 1.1

Child Care Food Program guidelines, 2.28
Child care network, benefits of,
4.52
Child care personnel, recognizing
child abuse or neglect, 5.17
Child care plans, roles of parents
in developing, 1.17
Child care policies: analyzing,
6.22; guidelines for, **33**
Child care programs: ages and
numbers of children in, 4.53;
children with special medical
and health-related needs, 1.11;
determining when a child is
ready to leave, 4.15, 4.29;
learning principles and goals,
1.3–1.4; serving children with
special needs, 1.10
Child care providers: defining
gaps in service and defining
responsibilities, **35**; low wages
of, **29**; role in ensuring quality
services, **20–21**
Child care records, 5.9–5.10;
confidentiality of, 5.10;
retention of, 5.10
Child care resource and referral
service, 6.1–6.26; clients
served by, 6.2; definition of,
6.1; delivering fair and equitable services, 6.10, 6.20
Child care service(s), **1**; accountability of, 5.20–5.21; advocacy
effort, 5.27; array of, **37**;
assumptions and values, **1–2**;
as child centered and family
focused, **22**; current, **21–25**;
ensuring access to consultants,
4.31; essential components of,
23–24; goals for, **22–23**; group
sizes, 4.54; health care of
children in, 2.1; implications
of recent trends and findings,
25–32; integration of all
components of, 4.32; making
available to all, **36**; manual,
5.8; policies and procedures for
emergency medical care, 2.12;

purpose of, **21–22**; range of
resources and facilities used
for, **24–25**; recognizing unmet
needs, **36**; responsibilities and
skills needed for various
positions in, 4.2; role in the
community approach, **20–21**;
safety and risk management
program, 2.18; size of, 4.52;
supporting parents, 1.19;
written agreement of responsibility with parents, 1.13
Child care service team, 4.16, 7.4
Child care standards, SSBG as the
focal point for, **6**
Child care subsidies, availability
of, 6.61
Child care subsidy systems, 6.56–
6.65; administrative issues of,
6.65; health and safety standards, 6.59; outreach and
public awareness by, 6.58;
payments from, 6.63; provider
reimbursement rates, 6.63;
providing supportive case
management services, 6.62;
technical assistance to providers, 6.64
Child care system, support
services, 6.1–6.65
Child Care WAGE$ Project, **29**
Child development associate
(CDA) certification, 4.2, 4.17
Child poverty rate, **11**
Child Protective Services (CPS),
215
Child welfare, **216**
Child well-being, **215–216**
Child c are providers. *See* Providers
Childhood, early, **218**
Childhood obesity, **30–31**
Child-parent relationship, primary
significance of, 4.1
Children: care of ill, 2.16; checking
for illness after absence, 2.16;
of color, **11**; with disabilities,
31; enrolling in subsidy
programs, 6.57; of incarcerated
parents, **14**; infected with HIV,

2.17; living in poverty, **10**; mental health of, **15**; physical activity of, 2.30; preschool-age, **213**; principles of grouping, 4.55; protective factors in, **16**; psychopathology in, **205**; regularly in nonparental care, **25**; school-age, **213**; with special needs, 1.1; staff providing services to, 6.55; of teen mothers, **15**; testing for HIV infection, 2.17; traits exhibited by resilient, **16–17**; universal needs of, **18–19**

Children's Foundation Child Care Licensing Study, **25**

Child-to-staff ratio, **215**. *See also* Ratio

Chilling, protecting children from, 2.16

Choices, skills for preschool-age children, 1.8

Civil Rights Act of 1964, Title VI, **12**

Code of ethics, for various professional disciplines, 4.38

Cognitive and language/literacy development, for preschool-age children, 1.8

Cognitive development: of infants, 1.6; of school-age children, 1.9; of toddlers, 1.7

Collaboration, **216**

Communicable diseases, 2.2, 2.16

Communication: cross-jurisdictional, 5.18; promoting provider/parent, 6.37, 6.47

Communities, **216**; as central to the health and well-being of children, **17–18**; mobilizing to support and strengthen families, **18**; recruiting staff from, 4.35; resource and referral core services to, 6.5; resource and referral service representing, 6.9; responsibility for children, **34**; responsibility for children and families, **17–21**

Community activities, for school-age children, 1.9

Community child care program, coordinated, 4.52

Community classes, 4.44

Community groups, working with, **36**

Community-based resource and referral services, 6.13

Community-based system for child care, **34–37**

Compensation packages, for child care providers, **29**

Competency-based staff development, 4.36

Component managers. *See* Managers

Comprehensive services: model for case management, 6.62; provided by the resource and referral service, 6.11

Computer technology, impact on child care providers, **29–30**

Concrete foundations, for playground equipment, 3.23

Conferences: attending local, regional, or national, 4.44; with parents, 1.18

Confidentiality, **216**; of information in child abuse cases, 5.18; of information in neglect cases, 5.18; policies on, 5.18; of records, 5.10; regarding HIV status of children, 2.17; of resource and referral service information, 6.14

Conflict-of-interest policy, 6.20

Consultants, 4.31

Contagious conditions, children with, 2.16

Contagious disease. *See* Communicable diseases

Continuing education, 4.2, 4.38

Continuity of care, 4.54, 6.42

Continuous quality improvement (CQI) program, 5.22, 5.23

events offered by, 6.51; staffing, 6.53–6.55; structure of, 6.27; training offered by, 6.46; transportation provided by, 6.43

Family child care providers: providing continuing family support, social services, and mental health services to, 7.5; responsibilities during enrollment and admission, 4.27; responsibilities for daily developmental learning activities, 4.24; responsibilities for evaluating a child's progress, 4.28; responsibilities in determining when a child is ready to leave, 4.29; responsibilities of, 4.23–4.29; responsibilities to the children, 4.25; responsibilities to the parents, 4.26; screening and selecting by family child care networks/ systems, 6.30. *See also* Care providers; Teacher/care provider

Family formations, **218**

Family foster care, **219**

Family home caregiver. *See* Small family child care home

Family resource, support, and education services, **219**

Family structure: change over the last three decades, **7–8**; division along ethnic lines, **8**

Family support, **204**; need for, 7.1; providing continuing, 7.2, 7.3, 7.5

Family Support Act (P.L. 100-485), **6**

Family support workers, 7.2, 7.4

Family-centered practice approach, **218**

Family-centered services, **218**

Fans, for playrooms, 3.35

Faucets, operation of, 3.9

FCC (Family child care), **218**

Federal child care standards, **3**

Federal government, role in child care services and subsidies, **5–7**

Federal income tax, dependent care credit, **32**

Federally funded child care subsidy system, 6.56

Feelings, preschool-age children talking about, 1.8

Fencing, of the outdoor play area, 3.22

Ferrets, 3.43

Fetal alcohol effect, **219**

Fetal alcohol syndrome, **219**

Financial assistance, assisting parents with finding, 6.3

Fingerprint and background investigation, of exempt providers, 6.59

Fire alarm system, in child care center buildings, 3.6

Fire departments, inspections by, 3.6

Fire drills, conducting, 2.23

Fire escapes, 3.6

Fire extinguishers, 3.6, 3.27

Fire inspections, for family and group child care homes, 3.27

Fire resistant material, in child care center buildings, 3.6

Firearms, in a family or group child care home, 3.41

Fires: open, 3.35; prohibited, 3.14

First aid supplies, keeping secure, 3.12

First-aid principles, 2.20

Flooring, of the playroom, 3.17, 3.38

Floors: in child care center buildings, 3.7; in family and group child care homes, 3.28

Food: allergies, 2.28; bringing from home, 2.29; cultural preferences, 2.28; encouraging children to try unfamiliar, 2.28

Food and Nutrition Service: Guidelines for the Child Care Food Program, 2.28; sanitation standards, 3.28

Food program enrollment, 6.48

Food storage facilities, 3.7, 3.28

members, 1.14; referring to providers, 6.34; resource and referral core services to, 6.3; respecting the standards and values of, 1.4; responsibilities of the family child care provider to, 4.26; role in developing individual child plans, 1.17; role in governance of the child case service, 5.19; role in preparing their child for new experiences, 1.16; role in quality programming, 1.12–1.20; special skills and talents of, 5.19; staff providing services to, 6.54; support services for, **2**; supporting, 1.19; teacher/care provider responsibilities to, 4.12; unlimited access to children, 6.60; working more hours per week, **9**

Parrot family (*psittacine*), birds of, 3.43

Peer mentors, for supervisors, 4.43

Peer review component, of continuous quality improvement, 5.23

Peer support meetings, 4.44

Pegboards, for toddlers, 1.7

Performance: objective measures of, 5.23; recognition of outstanding, 4.50

Periodic reviews, of child care records, 5.9

Permanency planning, **221**

Personal Responsibility and Work Opportunity Reconciliation Act (PRWORA), **6**, **10**

Personnel, for staff development and training, 4.37

Pervasive developmental disorder, **217**

Pesticides, avoiding exposure to, 3.7, 3.28

Pests, controlling, 3.7, 3.28

Pets: in the family or group child care home, 3.43; in the play space, 3.18

Physical abuse, **221**, 2.9

Physical access, to child care buildings and facilities, 3.3

Physical activity, allowing for daily, 2.30

Physical contact, positive for infants, 1.6

Physical development: of infants, 1.6; of preschool-age children, 1.8; of school-age children, 1.9; of toddlers, 1.7

Physical disabilities, access for children, families, staff, and visitors with, 3.3

Physical examinations: of family/group home child care providers, 4.30; special room for, 3.11; for staff, 2.13

Physical facilities, used for child care, 3.1–3.47

Physical interventions, objective observation of, **221**

Physical restraint, 5.15. *See also* Supportive holding

Physical safety, threats to teachers/care providers', 2.26

Physically challenged children, group sizes for, 4.57

Pillows, 2.15

Planned child-centered activities, 1.4

Plants: in the play space, 3.18; for preschool-age children, 1.8

Play, indispensable for young children, 1.1

Play space, in child care center buildings, 3.13–3.19

Playground area. *See* Outdoor play area

Playroom: arrangement of, 3.19, 3.40; equipment, 3.18; equipment, furnishings, and materials, 3.39; in family or group child care homes, 3.33–3.40; flooring, 3.17, 3.38; furnishings, 3.18; light and ventilation in, 3.15, 3.36; separating from the toilet facility, 3.9, 3.30; size of, 3.13, 3.34; soundproofing, 3.16, 3.37; temperature of, 3.14, 3.35; toilet and handwashing facilities, 3.9, 3.30